great
potato
recipes

mashed, baked and grilled:

great
potato
recipes

over 50 fabulous dishes
shown step-by-step

Sally Mansfield and Alex Barker

southwater

This edition is published by Southwater

Southwater is an imprint of Anness Publishing Ltd
Hermes House, 88–89 Blackfriars Road, London SE1 8HA
tel. 020 7401 2077; fax 020 7633 9499
www.southwaterbooks.com; info@anness.com

© Anness Publishing Ltd 2005

UK agent: The Manning Partnership Ltd
6 The Old Dairy, Melcombe Road, Bath BA2 3LR
tel. 01225 478444; fax 01225 478440
sales@manning-partnership.co.uk

UK distributor: Grantham Book Services Ltd
Isaac Newton Way, Alma Park Industrial Estate
Grantham, Lincs NG31 9SD
tel. 01476 541080; fax 01476 541061
orders@gbs.tbs-ltd.co.uk

North American agent/distributor: National Book Network
4501 Forbes Boulevard, Suite 200, Lanham, MD 20706
tel. 301 459 3366; fax 301 429 5746; www.nbnbooks.com

Australian agent/distributor: Pan Macmillan Australia
Level 18, St Martins Tower, 31 Market St, Sydney, NSW 2000
tel. 1300 135 113; fax 1300 135 103
customer.service@macmillan.com.au

New Zealand agent/distributor: David Bateman Ltd
30 Tarndale Grove, Off Bush Road, Albany, Auckland
tel. (09) 415 7664; fax (09) 415 8892

10 9 8 7 6 5 4 3 2 1

Publisher: Joanna Lorenz
Editorial Director: Judith Simons
Editors: Rebecca Clunes and Elizabeth Woodland
Designer: Margaret Sadler
Jacket Designer: Whitelight Design Associates
Photography: Steve Moss, Sam Stowell and Walt Chrynwski
Food for Photography: Alex Barker (techniques), Eliza Baird (recipes)
Additional Recipes: Roz Denny, Jacqueline Clarke, Joanna Farrow,
Shirley Gill, Sarah Gates, Steven Wheeler, Hilaire Walden,
Christine France, Rosamund Grant, Sheila Kimberley, Liz Trigg,
Carla Capalbo, Carole Clements, Judy Jackson, Ruby Le Bois,
Chris Ingram, Matthew Drennan, Elizabeth Wolfe-Cohen,
Shehzad Husain, Rafi Fernandez, Manisha Kanani, Laura Washburn,
Andi Clevely, Katherine Richmond, Jennie Shapter
Production Controller: Claire Rae

Previously published as part of a larger compendium,
  Discovering Potatoes

Picture Credits: E.T. Archive: page 6 (top and bottom), page 7 (top);
Illustrated London News: page 7 (bottom)

NOTES

Bracketed terms are intended for
American readers.

For all recipes, quantities are given in both
metric and imperial measures and, where
appropriate, measures are also given in
standard cups and spoons. Follow one set,
but not a mixture, because they are
not interchangeable.

Standard spoon and cup measures are level.
1 tsp = 5ml, 1 tbsp = 15ml,
1 cup = 250ml/8fl oz

Australian standard tablespoons are
20ml. Australian readers should use
3 tsp in place of 1 tbsp for measuring small
quantities of gelatine, flour, salt etc.

Medium (US large) eggs are used
unless otherwise stated.

CONTENTS

THE POTATO AND ITS HISTORY

THERE ARE FEW more important foods in the world than the potato. Its history goes back to the early days of man – a past spanning feast and famine. It has long played a vital role as the best all-round source of nutrition for mankind, and will continue to do so in the future.

The potato was discovered by pre-Inca Indians in the foothills of the Andes Mountains in South America. Archaeological remains have been found dating from 400 BC on the shores of Lake Titicaca, in ruins near Bolivia, and on the coast of Peru. Cultivated by the Incas, it influenced their whole lives. The Peruvian potato goddess was depicted holding a potato plant in each hand. The South American Indians measured time by the length of time it took to cook potatoes to various consistencies. Potato designs were found on Nazca and Chimu pottery. Raw slices of potato placed on broken bones were thought to prevent rheumatism.

The original potatoes, ranging from the size of a nut to a small apple, and ranging in colour from red and gold to blue and black, flourished in these temperate mountain plateaux. The first recorded information about the potato

was written in 1553 by the Spanish conquistador Pedro Cieza de Leon and soon potatoes joined the treasures carried away by these Spanish invaders. They became standard food on Spanish ships, and people began to notice that the sailors who ate them did not suffer from scurvy.

The first known purchase of the potato was by a hospital in Seville in 1573. Its cultivation spread quickly throughout Europe via explorers such as

Above: A ceramic plate made by the Incas, which typically would have been used for serving potatoes.

Sir Francis Drake, who is reputed to have brought potatoes back to Britain. These are thought to have been cultivated on Sir Walter Raleigh's estate in Ireland, 40,000 acres of land given to him by Queen Elizabeth I expressly to grow potatoes and tobacco. Botanists and scientists were fascinated by this novel plant – it was mentioned in John Gerard's herbal list in 1597 – and potatoes may first have been grown mainly for botanical research. During Charles II's reign, the Royal Society recognized the potato as being nutritional and inexpensive and, with the ever-present fear of war and famine, governments in Europe tried to persuade their farmers to start growing this valuable crop in quantity.

However the potato also carried with it a reputation. As part of the nightshade family, it was thought to be poisonous or to cause leprosy and syphilis and to be a dangerous aphrodisiac. In France, a young chemist, Antoine Augustin Parmentier, set about converting the French and their King Louis XVI with his potato delicacies (hence his name is now used often in connection with potato dishes), and Marie Antoinette was persuaded to wear potato blossoms in her hair. But in some cases it took more than just

Above: The Golden Hinde in which Sir Francis Drake brought potatoes back to Britain.

Above: The potato flower.

in the 1840s. Over a million people died and it is hardly surprising that the potato became known as the white or Irish potato, to distinguish it from the sweet potato.

The Irish took their love of the potato with them when they moved in large numbers to the north of England, as well as to Europe and America to escape the famine. The British government had by now accepted the potato as a nutritious, cheap and easily grown food and were encouraging the use of allotments for potato growing – "potato patches" as they became known in the Victorian era. The fear of another potato crop disaster through disease, along with the new-found appreciation of its table value caused intense interest in improving potato varieties throughout Europe. At the International Potato Show at London's Alexandra Palace in 1879 there were reputed to have been several hundred varieties on show. By the turn of the century the potato was the accepted main vegetable crop and was exported throughout Europe.

POTATOES IN THE WORLD TODAY

Now the potato is the staple food for two-thirds of the world's population and our third most important food crop. It is the best all-round source of nutrition known to man, second only to eggs for protein and better even than soya beans, the protein food of the second half of the 20th century. Growing potatoes is also the world's most efficient means of converting land, water and labour into an edible product – a field of potatoes produces more energy per acre per day than a field of any other crop.

persuasion. King Frederick of Prussia ordered his people to plant potatoes to prevent famine but had to enforce these orders by threatening to cut off the noses and ears of those who refused. European immigrants introduced potatoes to North America but it was not until Irish immigrants took the potato to Londonderry, New Hampshire, in 1719, that it began to be grown in any quantity. Early in the 19th century, Lord Selkirk also emigrated with a group from the Isle of Skye in Scotland to settle in an area known as Orwell Point on Prince Edward Island, Canada. With him he took potatoes and the community survived on potatoes and cod for many years.

By the end of the 18th century, the potato was becoming a major crop, particularly in Germany and Britain. The Irish peasants were eating a daily average of ten potatoes per person, 80 per cent of their diet. In addition, potatoes were fodder for their animals who provided their milk, meat and eggs. This total dependence proved to be disastrous for the Irish when the blight of *Phytophthora infestans* struck the potato harvest in three successive years

Above: The great exhibition hall at London's Alexandra Palace, where the International Potato Show was held in the 1800's.

PREPARATION TECHNIQUES

The method you use to prepare your potatoes affects the mineral and vitamin content, and the cooking technique.

CLEANING POTATOES

Most potatoes you buy today are very clean, especially those from supermarkets and pre-packed potatoes, so giving them a light wash will probably be sufficient before boiling them. Locally grown potatoes, farm shop or home-grown potatoes may still have some earth attached to them, so give them a light scrub before cooking. If you are not going to cook them immediately avoid scrubbing the potatoes with water as they can start to go mouldy in warm or damp weather.

1 If the potatoes are very dirty, use a small scrubbing brush or a gentle scourer to clean and remove the peel of the new potatoes.

2 Remove any green or discoloured patches or black eyes carefully, using a pointed knife or potato peeler, unless you are going to peel them after cooking, at which stage they will come out of their skins easily.

PEELING POTATOES

It is well known that much of the goodness and flavour of a potato is in the skin and just below it. You can boil the potatoes and then peel them afterwards when they are cool enough to handle. The taste is much fresher and earthier if they are prepared this way and perfect for eating plain or simply garnished. Leave the skins on occasionally, which gives more taste and added texture, plus a vital source of roughage and fibre to the diet. Save any peelings you have left over for a very healthy version of crisps (potato chips).

To peel potatoes use a very sharp potato peeler (there are many different varieties to choose from) to remove the thinnest layer possible in long even strips. Place the potatoes in a saucepan of water so they are just covered until ready to cook, but preferably cook them immediately to avoid any loss of vitamin C.

If you cook potatoes in their skins and want to peel them whilst hot ready for eating immediately, hold the hot potato with a fork and then gently peel off the skin – the skin tends to peel more easily while the potatoes are still hot.

SCRAPING POTATOES

Really new potatoes peel very easily, often just by rubbing them in your hands. You can tell a good new potato, when buying them, by how easily the skin rubs or flakes off.

With a small sharp knife scrape away the flaky skin and place in just enough water to cover.

RUMBLING

This wonderfully old-fashioned word refers to a catering machine with a large revolving bowl and rough, grater-like sides. The potatoes rumble around until the skins are eventually scratched or scraped off. There is one product available for the domestic market which peels the potatoes in the same way.

Wash the potatoes, place in the peeler drum with water as directed, then turn on to speed 2–3 and leave for several minutes. Remove any that are peeled and then continue until the rest are ready. Transfer to a pan of cold water ready for cooking. Don't put in more potatoes than recommended or they may come out misshapen.

GRATING BY HAND

Potatoes can be grated before or after cooking, depending on how you will be using them. They are easier to grate after cooking, when they have had time to cool, and can be grated on a large blade straight into the cooking dish or frying pan. Be sure you don't overcook the potatoes, especially if they are floury, as they will just fall to pieces. Floury potatoes are ideal for mashing, while waxy potatoes are a good choice for making rösti or hash.

Raw potatoes exude a surprising amount of starchy liquid that is vital to helping some dishes stick together. Check before you start whether you need to keep this liquid. The recipe should also tell you whether to rinse off the starchy liquid or just dry the potatoes on kitchen paper. Don't grate the potatoes too soon as the flesh quickly begins to turn brown.

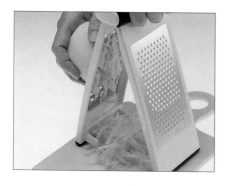

Using a standard grater, grate raw potatoes on a board.

Or if you need the liquid, grate into a medium bowl using either the medium or large blade. Squeeze the liquid from the potatoes by hand.

CHOPPING

Potatoes are often required to be chopped for recipes such as salads and dishes using leftovers. If you are cooking them first the best potatoes to choose are the waxy ones which stay nice and firm. They chop most easily when they are cold and peeled.

To chop, cut the potato in half, then half again and again until it is cut up evenly, as small as is required.

DICING

If the recipe calls for dice this means you have to be much more precise and cut the potato into even shaped cubes. This is usually so that all the sides brown neatly or the pieces cook through evenly.

1 To dice, trim the potato into a neat rectangle first (keep the outside pieces for mash, or to add to a soup), then cut the rectangles into thick, even slices.

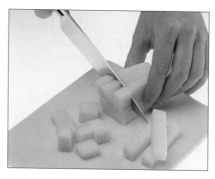

2 Turn the stack of slices over and cut into thick batons and finally into even cubes of the size needed for the recipe you are using.

SLICING BY HAND

It may not always matter how neatly and evenly you slice your potatoes, but for some dishes it will affect both the appearance of the finished dish and the cooking time. Try to cut all slices the same thickness so that they cook evenly. Use a large knife for the best results, and make sure that it is sharp otherwise it may slip and cause a nasty cut. To make rounder slices cut across the width of the potato, for longer slices cut along the length of the potato. If you need to slice cooked potatoes for a recipe, be sure to slightly undercook them so they don't fall to pieces either in the dish or when slicing, and let them get really cold before handling them. For most casseroles and toppings cut them about 3mm/⅛in thick.

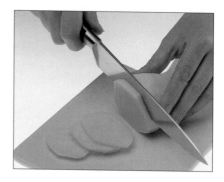

Put the tip of the knife on the work surface or board first, then press the heel of the knife down firmly to create nice even slices.

SLICING WITH A MANDOLINE

A relative of the musical instrument of the same name, the mandoline has several different cutting blades which vary both the size and shape of the cut potato. The blades are fitted into a metal, plastic or wooden framework for ease of use. It can produce slices from very thin to very thick, as well as fluted slices for crinkle-cut style crisps (potato chips). It's quite a dangerous gadget, and needs handling with respect because of its very sharp blades. You can cut different thicknesses as required, such as, medium thick (about 2–3mm/$\frac{1}{16}$–$\frac{1}{8}$in) for sautéed potato slices and very thin for crisps.

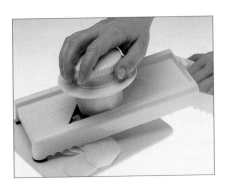

Plain Slices

Fix the blade to the required thickness, then, holding the potato carefully, slide it firmly up and down or across the blade. Use the handle or gadget that is provided with some versions to hold on to whenever possible.

Crinkle-cut

For crinkle-cut slices cut the potato horizontally down the fluted blade. Take particular care when the potato gets smaller as it is easy to cut one's fingers on the blade.

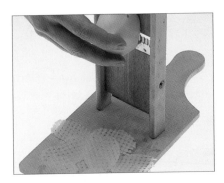

Waffled Crisps

For the fancy waffled crisps (*pomme gaufrettes*), cut horizontally down the blade, rotating each time you slice to get a lattice effect.

MAKING CRISPS (CHIPS) BY HAND

Home-made crisps are the best, but they can be very fiddly if you do not have the right tools for making them. For a large batch slice the potatoes in a food processor, but for a small batch the slicing blade on a standard grater should give thin enough potato slices if you use it carefully. You can also use a sharp knife to make crisps, but you need to be very careful.

Grating Crisps

To make thin crisps, hold a standard grater firmly on a chopping board, placing a damp cloth on the board to anchor the grater to it and prevent it from sliding. Slide the potato down over the slicing blade carefully. Be sure the grater or mandoline has a very sharp blade. Adjust it to the right thickness or, if it's not adjustable, you will find that the harder you press, the thicker the crisps will be.

Slicing Crisps

This method is best if you want to make small quantites of thick crisps. Hold one end of the potato firmly in your hand and cut thin slices – 3mm/$\frac{1}{8}$in thick – with a sharp knife, on a chopping board. Slicing crisps with a knife means that it is easier to adjust the thickness. Remember that the thicker the slice, the less oil will be absorbed by the potato during cooking.

MAKING RIBBONS BY HAND

Thin ribbons, which also deep fry into delicious crisps, can be simply cut with a potato peeler. (Any leftover odd shapes can go into the stockpot.)

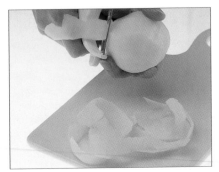

To make ribbons, peel the potato like an apple to give very long strips. Work quickly, or put the ribbons in a bowl of cold water as you go, to prevent them turning brown.

CHIPS (FRENCH FRIES)

The French give their chips various names, depending on how thin or thick they are cut. The larger you cut them the healthier they will be, since they will absorb less fat during the cooking. You can also make chips with their skins on, giving additional fibre.

Traditional

Use the largest suitable potatoes and cut the potatoes into 1.5cm/⅝in thick slices, or thicker if you wish.

Turn the slices on their side and cut into 1.5cm/⅝in batons, or slightly thicker or thinner if you prefer.

Wedges

For a healthier alternative cut your chips, extra thick, into wedge shapes. First cut the potatoes in half lengthways, then into long thin wedges.

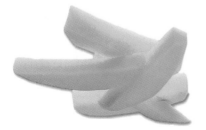

Pommes Frites

Cut as for chips but slice again into neat, even batons about 6mm/⅓in thick, either by hand or machine.

Pommes Allumettes

Cut the potato into a neat rectangle by removing the rounded sides, then into thin slices and julienne strips about half the thickness of *pommes frites*.

Pommes Pailles

Cut the potatoes as for *pommes allumettes* into even finer julienne strips. They are usually pan fried.

Cutter Chips

Chips can be cut with a special chip cutter (see equipment section) and some mandolines. Cut the potatoes to a suitable size to fit.

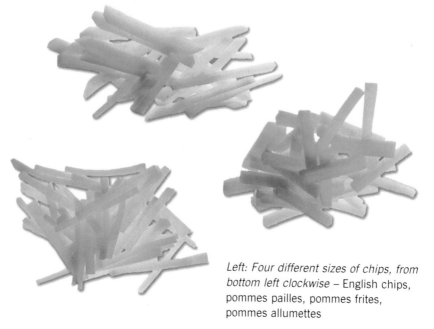

Left: Four different sizes of chips, from bottom left clockwise – English chips, pommes pailles, pommes frites, pommes allumettes

HASSELBACK AND FAN POTATOES

Children often refer to these as hedgehogs as they look quite spiky when roasted to a crispy, golden brown. Peel and dry the potatoes then slice as shown, brush with oil and then put them to roast as soon as possible before they begin to discolour.

To make hasselback potatoes, cut large potatoes in half and place cut side down on a board. With a sharp knife, cut very thin slices across the potato from end to end, slicing deep but not quite through the potato.

To make potato fans, use medium potatoes of long or oval shape and cut them at a slight angle, slicing almost but not quite through the potato, keeping the back section still attached. Press the potato gently on the top until it flattens and fans out at the same time. If you have not cut far enough through it will not fan very much, but if you have cut too far it will split into sections. The best way to cook both these potatoes is to cook them with melted butter and oil and roast them in the oven, preheated to 190°C/375°F/Gas 5, for 40–50 minutes.

SHAPED POTATOES

Occasionally it is fun to spend the time making potatoes into an artistic creation. You might try these out with children when you are encouraging them to get more involved with preparing and cooking family meals. Use the offcuts for making mash or to thicken soups.

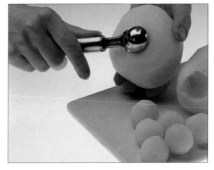

To make potato balls use large firm potatoes for the best results. Peel them and then using a large round or shaped melon baller push it firmly into the potato, twist, and ease out the potato shape. Keep in water until ready to cook, pat dry on kitchen paper and roast or sauté as usual.

To make turned potatoes, first peel small to medium firm potatoes (or quartered large potatoes), trim the ends flat and then cut or trim with a small knife into barrel shapes 2.5–5cm/1–2in long.

To make potato wedges, cut potatoes in half lengthways, then into quarters and then into eighths. Brush with oil and oven roast or deep fry. The larger the pieces of potato the less fat they will absorb.

PREPARING POTATOES BY MACHINE

Some machines will do many of the jobs already mentioned, such as peeling, grating, slicing, chipping and puréeing, with great speed but not with the precision of your own hands. To get the best results, always cut the potatoes to the same size, use the slowest speed or pulse so you can control the results, and cook the cut potatoes immediately or rinse and dry on kitchen paper to prevent browning.

Home-cooked chips (french fries) are always the best kind, and cutting them by hand can be time consuming. So use a machine to prepare them for cooking. Fit the correct blade attachment and pack sufficient potatoes in the tube of the food processor so they can be pushed down. Turn on to the slowest speed and press the potato down with the plunger. The harder you press the plunger the thicker the chips will be.

They may turn out slightly bent but that won't affect the taste. For nice evenly sliced potatoes change the attachment on the machine and pack the potatoes so that they will remain facing the same direction and continue as above.

COOKING TECHNIQUES

There are endless different ways of cooking potatoes. However, the best technique depends on both the potato variety and the dish you are cooking.

BLANCHING

Potatoes are blanched (part-cooked) to soften the skin for easy peeling, to remove excess starch for certain recipes and to par-cook before roasting. Use a draining spoon or basket to remove large pieces of potato but when cooking smaller potatoes, place the potatoes in a chip basket for easy removal.

Place the prepared potatoes in a pan of cold water. Bring slowly to the boil and boil gently for 2–5 minutes depending on their size, then drain and use or leave in the cooling water until required.

BOILING

This is the simplest way of cooking potatoes. Place potatoes of a similar size, either whole or cut into chunks, with or without skins (sweet potatoes are best cooked in their skins to retain their bright colour) in a pan with sufficient water just to cover them. Sprinkle on 5–10ml/1–2 tsp salt or to taste, and bring slowly to the boil. Floury potatoes need very gentle boiling or you may find the outside is cooked before the inside is ready and they will become mushy or fall apart in the pan. New potatoes, which have a higher vitamin C content, should be put straight into boiling water and cooked for about 15 minutes and not left soaking. Very firm salad potatoes can be put into boiling water, simmered for

5–10 minutes and then left to stand in the hot water for another 10 minutes until required.

1 Place the potatoes in a large pan and just cover with salted water and a tight-fitting lid. Bring to the boil and leave to gently boil for 15–20 minutes depending on the size and type of potato. Boiling too fast tends to cook the potato on the outside first so it becomes mushy and falls apart before the middle is cooked.

2 When they are finished cooking, drain the potatoes through a colander and then return them to the pan to dry off, as wet or soggy potatoes are not very appetizing.

3 For really dry, peeled potatoes (for mashing for instance), leave them over a very low heat so any moisture can escape. In the north of England they sprinkle the potatoes with salt and shake occasionally until the potatoes stick to the sides of the pan.

4 In Ireland the potatoes are wrapped in a clean tea towel until ready to serve dry and fluffy.

STEAMING

All potatoes steam well but this gentle way of cooking is particularly good for very floury potatoes and those which fall apart easily. Small potatoes, such as new potatoes, steamed in their skins taste really delicious. Make sure potatoes are cut quite small, in even-size chunks or thick slices. Leaving cooked potatoes over a steaming pan of water is also a good way to keep them warm for several minutes.

1 Place prepared potatoes in a sieve (strainer), colander or steamer over a deep pan of boiling salted water. Cover as tightly as possible and steam for 5–7 minutes if sliced or cut small, increasing the time to 20 minutes or more if the potatoes are quite large.

2 Towards the end of the cooking time, test a few of the potatoes with a sharp knife, and when cooked, turn off the heat and leave until you are ready to serve them.

3 As an alternative, place a handful of fresh mint leaves in the bottom of the steamer before cooking. The flavour of the mint will penetrate during cooking.

FRYING

The key to successful frying is good fat. A mixture of butter and oil gives good flavour yet allows a higher cooking temperature than just butter.

Shallow-frying

Use a large, heavy frying pan to allow an even distribution of heat and sufficient room to turn the food.

1 Heat about 25g/1oz/2 tbsp butter and 30ml/2 tbsp oil until bubbling. Put an even layer of cooked or par-cooked potatoes in the hot fat taking care not to splash yourself. Leave for 4–5 minutes until the undersides turn golden.

2 Turn the potatoes over gently with a large spatula once or twice during cooking until golden brown all over.

Deep-frying

When deep-frying, whether you use oil or solid fat, be sure it is fresh and clean. The chips must be well dried as water can cause the fat to bubble up dangerously. Always fry in small batches so the temperature does not drop too much when you add the food and it can cook and brown evenly. Remove any burnt pieces after each batch as this can taint the fat.

To deep fry potatoes, fill either a deep heavy pan with tight-fitting lid, or a deep-fat fryer, about half full with clean fat. Heat to the required temperature by setting the thermostat or test if the oil is hot enough by dropping in a piece of bread; it should turn golden in one minute.

When making chips (french fries) they are best "blanched" first in hot fat to cook through and seal them without browning. These can then be removed, drained and frozen when cool. Give them a final cooking when you are almost ready to eat, to crisp them up and turn them golden brown.

1 Before frying, dry the potatoes very thoroughly in a cloth or kitchen paper. Any water or moisture will make the fat splash and spit.

2 Heat the basket in the fat first, then add the potatoes to the basket (don't overfill or they will not cook evenly), and lower slowly into the pan. If the fat appears to bubble up too much remove the basket and cool the fat slightly.

3 Shake the pan of chips occasionally to allow even cooking, and cook until they are crisp and golden. Remove with a draining spoon or wire basket and drain well against the side of the pan first.

4 Tip the chips on to kitchen paper to get rid of the excess fat before serving, sprinkled with salt.

Deep-frying temperatures

- To blanch and seal chips 160°C/325°F
- To quickly fry fine straw chips and crisps (potato chips) and to second cook chips 190°C/375°F

Potato Baskets

1 Cut potatoes into thin, even slices and dry on kitchen paper without rinsing. You will need two wire potato baskets or ladles. Line the larger one evenly with overlapping slices, covering the base well, then clamp the smaller basket inside this one.

2 Slowly immerse in very hot fat for 3–4 minutes until starting to turn golden brown.

3 Remove from the heat, separate the ladles and ease out the basket. Drop back into the fat for another 1–2 minutes until golden.

4 Serve filled with vegetables, stir-fried meat, or sweet and sour prawns (shrimp).

Safe deep-frying

- Never overfill the pan, with either fat or food.
- Always use a tight-fitting lid.
- Have ready a large, very thick cloth to throw over the pan in case of fire.
- NEVER throw water on to a chip pan full of hot or burning fat as it will explode.

BAKING

One of the most comforting and economical meals is a salt-crusted potato baked in its jacket with a fluffy centre that is golden with melted butter and cheese.

Sweet potatoes can be cooked in exactly the same way, sprinkled with a little demerara sugar and topped with sour cream and crispy bacon.

Allow a 275–350g/10–12oz potato for a good size portion and choose the ones recommended for baking, such as Marfona, Maris Piper, Cara or King Edward. Cook in the middle of a hot oven at 220ºC/425ºF/Gas 7 for 1–1½ hours for very large potatoes or 40–60 minutes for medium potatoes. To test that they are cooked, squeeze the sides gently to make sure that they are sufficiently soft.

1 Wash and dry baking potatoes thoroughly then rub with good oil and add a generous sprinkling of salt. Cook on a baking tray as above.

2 To speed up cooking time and to ensure even cooking throughout, cook the baking potatoes on a skewer, or on special potato baking racks.

3 When really tender cut a cross in the top of each potato and set aside to cool slightly.

4 Hold the hot potato in a clean cloth and squeeze gently from underneath to open up.

5 Place the open potatoes on individual serving plates and pop a lump of butter in each one.

6 For a quick and simple topping, add a little grated tangy Cheddar or similar hard cheese, or a dollop of sour cream and some chopped fresh herbs, such as chives, parsley or coriander (cilantro). Season with plenty of salt and ground black pepper.

Baked Potato Skins

Bake the potatoes at 220ºC/425ºF/Gas 7 for 1–1½ hours for large potatoes and 40–60 minutes for medium. Cut in half and scoop out the soft centres. (Mash for a supper or a pie topping.)

Brush the skins with melted butter, margarine or a mixture of butter and oil and return to the top of the oven, at the same temperature, for 20 minutes or until really crisp and golden.

Potato Parcels

Baking a potato in a foil or baking parchment parcel, or in a roasting bag, makes for a very tasty potato with no mess and no dirty dishes, if you're careful. If you leave the potatoes in their skins you could prepare them well in advance and put them in to cook in an automatic oven before you get home.

Wash or scrub and dry small potatoes, then wrap them up in a parcel with several knobs (pats) of butter, a sprinkle of seasoning and a sprig or two of mint, tarragon or chives. Bake at 190ºC/ 375ºF/Gas 5 for about 40–50 minutes for 450g/1lb potatoes.

COOKING IN A CLAY POT

This is most like cooking in a bonfire or under a pile of earth – but here the potatoes take on a deep woody aroma and intense flavour without all the charring and smoke. The terracotta potato pot takes a generous 450g/1lb of potatoes easily. As with all clay pot utensils it should be soaked for 10–20 minutes before using. Use small, even-size potatoes, preferably in their skins. Always place the pot in a cold oven and let the temperature gradually increase to 200°C/400°F/Gas 6. Cook for 40–50 minutes and then test with a pointed knife to see if they are ready.

1 Put the prepared potatoes in the clay pot, toss in 30–45ml/2–3 tbsp of good, preferably extra virgin olive oil or melted butter and sprinkle with roughly ground salt from a mill and pepper. Add your favourite flavourings, such as one large unpeeled clove of garlic, a thick piece of streaky (fatty) smoked bacon, chopped, or fresh herbs.

2 Put the covered pot in the cold oven and allow to heat to 200°C/400°F/Gas 6. After 40–50 minutes test with a knife. Serve straight from the pot.

MICROWAVED POTATOES

Baking potatoes in the microwave is an enormous time saver, as long as you don't expect the crunchy crust of oven-cooked potatoes. New potatoes and potato pieces can be cooked very quickly and easily. In both cases prick the potato skins first, to prevent bursting. To bake, allow 4–6 minutes per potato, with the setting on a high temperature, increasing by 2–4 minutes for every additional potato. As a guide for smaller boiled potatoes, allow 10–12 minutes per 450g/1lb of cut potatoes on high, or follow the manufacturer's instructions.

Place large potatoes in a circle on kitchen paper on the microwave tray, make cuts around the middle so the skins don't burst and turn once during the cooking process.

Place small potatoes in a microwave bowl with 30–45ml/2–3 tbsp boiling water. Cover tightly with microwave film and pierce two or three times to allow steam to escape during cooking. Leave for 3–5 minutes before draining, adding a knob (pat) or two of butter, seasoning and a sprig of mint.

Alternatively, cover the potatoes with a close-fitting microwave lid and cook them using the same method as for the microwave film covered bowl.

> **Standing time**
>
> Allow sufficient standing time afterwards so the potatoes are evenly cooked. Large, baked potatoes should be left to stand for 10 minutes wrapped in napkins. This will keep them warm before serving and ensure even cooking.

PRESSURE-COOKING

If you want baked potatoes or large potatoes to be cooked in a hurry, or if you want to make a quick and easy mash, this is an ideal cooking method, but it's important to make sure you do not to overcook them, otherwise the potatoes will become dry and floury. Follow the instructions in your manual and allow up to 12 minutes cooking time for large whole potatoes; less for smaller ones. You can cook the potatoes in their skins, which speeds up the process further. Once the potatoes are ready, carefully reduce steam pressure so that they do not overcook.

ROASTING

Melt-in-the-mouth roast potatoes are always a popular choice, so here are some pointers to make sure you get them right every time.

For soft, fluffy-centred roast potatoes, you need to use large baking potatoes – Wilja, Maris Piper, Record, Désirée and Kerr's Pink all give excellent results. Peel (you can roast potatoes in their skins but you won't get the crunchy result most people love), and cut into even-size pieces. Blanch for 5 minutes, then leave in the cooling water for a further 5 minutes to par-cook evenly. Drain well and return to the pan to dry off completely. Well-drained potatoes with roughed up surfaces produce the crispiest results.

A successful roast potato also depends on the fat you cook them in and the temperature. Beef dripping gives the best flavour, although goose fat, if you are lucky enough to find some, is delicious and gives a very light, crisp result. With other roasts you can use lard or, where possible, drain off enough dripping from the joint. A vegetarian alternative is a light olive oil, or olive and sunflower oils mixed.

The fat in the roasting pan must be hot enough to seal the potato surfaces immediately. Use a large enough pan so that you have room to turn the potatoes at least once. Don't leave the almost cooked potatoes in too much fat as they will become soggy. Serve as soon as they are ready for maximum crispness.

1 Blanch the peeled chunks of potato and drain, then shake in the pan or fork over the surfaces to rough them up.

2 Pour a shallow layer of your chosen fat into a good heavy roasting pan and place it in the oven, heating it to a temperature of 220°C/425°F/Gas 7. Add the dry, forked potatoes and toss immediately in the hot oil. Return to the top shelf of the oven and roast for up to one hour.

3 Once or twice during cooking remove the roasting pan from the oven and, using a spatula, turn the potatoes over to evenly coat them in fat. Then drain off any excess fat so they can crisp up and brown more easily.

Seasoning

Flavourings you could try are:
- Curry powder mixes.
- Ground hazelnuts or other nuts.
- Dry seasoning mixes such as Italian Garlic Seasoning or Cajun Seasoning.
- Sesame seeds.
- Garlic and herb breadcrumbs.
- Grated Parmesan cheese.

Healthy Wedges

As a healthier alternative to deep-fried or roasted potatoes, serve wedges of dry-roasted potatoes sprinkled with various seasonings. Bake at 190°C/375°F/ Gas 5, turning often until golden and crisp.

1 Cut large baking potatoes into long thin wedges. Toss in a small amount of very hot sunflower oil in a roasting pan.

2 Sprinkle on seasonings, turn the wedges over several times and bake for 30–40 minutes, turning and testing once or twice.

MASHING AND PURÉEING

The ubiquitous mashed potato has seen a revival in recent years, from a favourite comfort food into a fashion food purely by the addition of olive oil or Parmesan cheese. Every chef and every trendy restaurant today produces their own version. It shows what can be done with a simple ingredient, but you've got to start with good mash. When choosing your potatoes remember that floury potatoes produce a light fluffy mash, while waxy potatoes will result in a dense, rather gluey purée which needs lots of loosening up. Boil even-size potatoes until very well cooked but not falling apart and dry them well, as watery potatoes will give a soggy, heavy mixture. Cold potatoes mash best of all. Sweet potatoes also mash well, to serve as a savoury or sweet dish.

You can mash potatoes in several ways: using a hand masher, which gives a very smooth result; pressing the potatoes through a ricer, sieve (strainer) or food mill, which gives a very light and fluffy result; using a fork, which can result in a slightly lumpy, uneven mixture; or using a pestle-type basher. An electric hand-held mixer can be used but don't be tempted to blend or purée them in the food processor as the end product will be a very solid, gluey mixture, ideal for turning into soup.

Making Mashed Potatoes

There are a number of different hand mashers available for sale but the best ones are those that have a strong but open cutting grid. Simply push down on the cooked potatoes, making sure you cover every area in the pan, and you will get a smooth, yet textured result.

Press potatoes through a ricer for an easy way to prepare light and fluffy mash. For a low-calorie side dish, press the potatoes straight into a heated bowl.

Alternatively beat in a generous knob (pat) of butter, some full cream (whole) milk, then season to taste, and mash until you have a creamy, fluffy mixture.

Quick Toppings

There are many simple ways to make mashed potatoes look more exciting and even tempt youngsters to try something new and unusual.

Rough up the topping on a shepherd's pie by running a fork through it.

An alternative decorative effect can be created using the back of a spoon to gently swirl the potato into soft hollows and peaks.

For a more chunky topping, use two matching spoons to make scoops or quenelle shapes, carefully moulding the potato around the sides of the spoons.

A quick and easy pattern to achieve is a lattice design. Run with a fork up and down the pie topping, before brushing with egg and then placing under a pre-heated grill (broiler) to brown.

Piping Mashed Potatoes

Smooth and creamy mashed potatoes will pipe beautifully, and your results can look professional with very little practice. But it does have to be really smooth mash, since any lumps will ruin your efforts and may clog up the piping bag and nozzle. Place a large, star nozzle in a large clean piping (pastry) bag and using a spoon fill the bag two-thirds with mash. Use your left hand to hold and guide the nozzle and your right hand to squeeze the potato down the bag. Practise a few times on a board, doing it slowly at first.

Duchesse Potatoes and Rosettes

These are the fancy portions which are often served in hotels. Rosettes are piped on to baking trays, brushed with beaten egg and baked until just golden to serve as a vegetable accompaniment to a main meal. They are very easy to make at home, however, if you want to impress your friends at a dinner party. You will need to use a firmer mashed potato than normal. To do this simply add egg yolks instead of milk to the potatoes in the pan and combine well. Brush with an egg glaze: 1 small egg, beaten with 15–30ml/1–2 tbsp water will give a thin mixture. Bake at 190°C/375°F/Gas 5 until golden brown.

1 Place a large, clean piping bag, fitted with a star nozzle, in a jar to hold it steady. Spoon in the thickened mashed potato until the bag is two-thirds full.

2 Start by squeezing out a small circle of potato, moving the nozzle slowly in one direction.

3 Then, still squeezing gently, fill in the centre and lift the bag up to make a cone shape.

Piped Topping

1 The same shape as above, made with a smaller nozzle, can be used to give a pie a very professional topping.

2 Bake the topping in the oven, preheated to 190°C/375°F/Gas 5 for 10-15 minutes, or grill (broil) for 5 minutes.

Potato Nests

These make a great meal for young children or an attractive dish for dinner. Fill with asparagus spears, fresh peas, corn, baked beans, soft cheese, chicken, fish or mushrooms in a creamy sauce and heat through.

1 Using the same nozzle as for duchesse potatoes pipe a large circle, or oval, on to a baking sheet or on to baking parchment.

2 Then fill in the base and pipe over the outer circle again to give height to the sides. Glaze and bake as for duchesse potatoes.

Piped Edgings

Many dishes can have piped potato edges. Most well known is the individual appetizer Coquilles St Jacques, where the potato holds the fish and creamy sauce safely in the scallop shell.

Pipe a circle, just like the potato nests, but around the edge of a cleaned scallop shell or a china version of this. Brush with egg, fill with fish mixture and then grill (broil) until golden.

Mashed Potato Flavours

To make a Mediterranean version beat in salt, pepper and good-quality olive oil to give a smooth soft mixture. Serve sprinkled with plenty of finely grated Parmesan cheese.

To make a wickedly rich mash, add thick cream or crème fraîche and grated fresh nutmeg. Mix thoroughly and serve with more grated nutmeg.

To make a lovely creamy mixture, beat in good, preferably extra virgin, olive oil and enough hot milk to make a smooth, thick purée. Then flavour to taste with salt and ground black pepper and stir in a few fresh basil leaves or parsley sprigs, chopped.

Chopped, cooked cabbage, spring onions (scallions) and leeks are all regional favourites which add lots of flavour to a family supper dish.

Try a spicy mixture of chilli powder, or very finely chopped chilli and chives to sprinkle over a creamy mash.

To make a crunchy texture, place a few bacon rashers (strips) under a hot grill (broiler) and once they are nice and crispy, chop them up and sprinkle over the potato.

To make a nutty mash, try toasted, flaked (sliced) almonds or roughly chopped nuts of your choice.

USING COOKED POTATOES

Potatoes are one of the most versatile leftovers to have in the fridge, so it is well worth cooking extra when you make them, especially if a member of the family cannot tolerate wheat or cereals. You can use mashed potatoes in fish cakes, to thicken soups or stews, to make breads and scones and for a very light pastry to use in traditional savoury dishes or quiches. Grated, cooked potato can be used for rösti, hashes, omelettes, tortillas, and even to beef up a salad.

Potato Pastry

1 Rub 100g/4oz/8 tbsp dripping, lard or butter into 450g/1lb/4 cups sifted plain (all-purpose) flour and add 450g/1lb mashed potatoes, 10ml/2 tsp salt, 1 beaten egg and sufficient milk so that when you draw the mixture together it is smooth but firm. Chill the pastry in the refrigerator for 10 minutes before use.

2 Roll the pastry out on a floured surface to an even thickness and use to line a suitable dish or baking pan. Chill the pastry in the dish again for 1 hour before pricking the bottom and filling as you wish.

Potato Croquettes

1 Enrich a firm mash with egg, as for duchesse potatoes, season or add flavourings to taste, then shape into small cylinders, rolling out with a little flour to prevent sticking.

2 Brush lightly with beaten egg, then coat or dip into any favourite mixture, like flaked almonds or grated cheese mixed with breadcrumbs.

3 Shallow fry in butter and oil, turning occasionally until golden brown and warmed through. Croquettes can also be deep fried, or baked until golden brown. (Try putting a nugget of cheese in the middle before cooking for a delicious appetizer or supper dish.)

Rösti

1 Grate cold, parboiled, waxy potatoes, on the largest side of a grater into a bowl and season to taste.

2 Heat a mixture of butter and oil in a heavy non-stick pan and, when bubbling, put in spoonfuls of the grated potato and flatten down neatly. Cook over low to medium heat until the rösti are golden and crisp underneath, which takes about 7–10 minutes.

3 Turn each of the rösti over with a fish slice, taking care that they do not fall apart, and continue cooking for another 5 minutes or until really crisp.

4 To prepare one large rösti, spoon the potato mixture into the bubbling fat, flatten out evenly and leave to cook over a medium heat for about 10 minutes or until turning golden underneath. To turn the rösti over easily invert it on to a large plate – use a plate that fits right into the pan over the potato.

5 Turn the pan and plate over carefully so that the rösti slips on to the plate without breaking up.

6 Gently slide it back into the pan, with an extra knob (pat) of butter if necessary. Continue cooking for another 10 minutes or until crisp underneath. Serve cut into generous slices.

BUYING AND STORING

Now that there is such a variety of potatoes to choose from, suited for every kind of cooking, it is important to think about how you plan to use your potatoes before you shop for them.

BUYING

Being tempted by some lovely little creamy potatoes, when what you want to make is a velvety thick soup or the topping for a shepherd's pie, won't give you complete success. Look at the Potato Index so you can choose the right variety for your menu. If you like to eat the skins and are concerned about what may be sprayed on them, then you would be well-advised to buy organic potatoes. Or you might consider growing your own – a very easy and rewarding task if you have the space.

When buying new potatoes check that they are really young and fresh by scraping the skin, which should peel off easily. New potatoes have a high vitamin C content so buy and eat them as fresh as possible for maximum goodness.

Maincrop potatoes should be firm. Avoid any which are soft, flabby, sprouting or have a white dusty mould.

Check for any green patches. These are a sign that the potatoes have been stored in the light and, although the rest of the potato is fine to eat, you do need to cut out these poisonous patches.

STORING

Potatoes have come from the dark and like to stay in the dark, and they do not keep too well unless carefully stored. In the warmth of a centrally heated kitchen they can start sprouting; the dampness of a cold fridge will make them sweaty and mouldy, and in too much light they begin to lose their nutritional value and start turning green. New potatoes in particular should be eaten within two or three days, to prevent mould forming on the surface. Unless they can be kept in the dark, it is better to buy in small quantities, a few pounds at a time, so that they are used quickly.

If you prefer to buy your potatoes in bulk, by the sack or in a large paper bag, then you need to find a dark, dry larder or garage, where they won't freeze in cold weather but the temperature is low enough not to encourage the growth of any sprouts.

If you are storing your potatoes in the house, put them into an open storage rack or basket or a well aerated bin in a dry, dark room.

When you buy potatoes in plastic bags remove them from the bags immediately you get them. Then store them in a suitable place.

Read the storage and keeping times of pre-packed potatoes, since these come in many varieties. Some are ready to cook, and others are already peeled or cleaned. You can even buy potatoes with seasonings or flavoured butter nowadays, but these are best consumed soon after purchasing; again read the packet for correct storage times.

PLANNING AHEAD

If you like to be organized and peel potatoes in advance – don't. Storing peeled potatoes in water will remove almost every trace of vitamin C. Even storing them tightly covered but without water in the refrigerator will result in nasty black potatoes.

A much better option is to almost fully cook the potatoes in their skins, leaving them very firm. They can be refrigerated like this, covered, for 2–3 days. Then when you come to use them, peel and chop the potatoes and reheat in the microwave or cook for a further 3–5 minutes with mint, or use as you would normally in a recipe. You should also find that they have far more flavour.

You can store already mashed potato covered with clear film (plastic wrap) ready to make into rissoles or toppings.

FREEZING POTATOES

Raw potato does not freeze at all well as it goes mushy, but cooked potato freezes quite well, although it has a tendency to go watery, so make sure it is very well dried before freezing.

Pipe duchesse potatoes or rosettes on to a baking tray, freeze until hard and store in a container. Cook from frozen.

Croquettes, rissoles, potato cakes and rösti should be individually wrapped or separated by baking parchment and then packed in fours or eights. Partly defrost them if they contain any meat or fish, then cook as for the original recipe.

Chips (french fries) can be cooked but not browned, ready for a last minute really hot fry to crisp them. Freeze them on trays and then transfer to bags. Partly defrost on kitchen paper before deep-frying in small batches.

POTATO PRODUCTS

There are many forms of prepared potato available in the shops today. Instant mashed potato, in powder or flake form, is very easy to use and now comes with popular flavour additions; potato flour makes a healthy alternative to wheat, and canned new potatoes mean a salad is made in seconds. Foil pouches contain ready-to-fry potato suppers with a very long shelf life, and an array of seasonings could give your baked potatoes, slices or wedges a welcome spark of flavour.

EQUIPMENT

The right piece of equipment for the job always makes life easier and you may find that there are now gadgets available that you haven't come across. Some tools, like potato peelers, become old friends too. If you are used to using one particular style you will be loath to change. Just glancing at the selection of equipment now available, it's difficult to know where to start. If you could try out a gadget before buying it, like trying on clothes, you would have an easier time choosing the right one. This list is designed to help.

Above: Lancashire peelers.

Peelers

Lancashire peeler This is the most traditional peeler, with a solid handle, often made from wood and string, and a rigid blade. They are firm and last well and also double up as a corer.

Stainless steel peeler Lightweight and inexpensive. The sharpest ones will give the thinnest peel. Beware the very cheap ones with stainless steel blades that bend, snap or blunt very quickly.

Above: Stainless steel peeler.

Swivel-blade peeler These are for left- or right-handed people, but they are not very strong for heavy-duty work.

The horizontal-angled blades are fast and easy to use on large potatoes.
Peeler with brush For dirty work you could try a swivel-blade peeler with brush attached.

Thick-grip peeler Many peelers now have good, thick grips which make light work of any peeling job and are much easier on the muscles for those with arthritic problems.

Twin-bladed peeler Takes a little time getting used to, but if you are preparing large quantities of big potatoes you could be grateful for this efficiency.

Coloured peeler Modern kitchen colours are now echoed in the design of kitchen equipment such as peelers, but following the trend doesn't always produce quality products. Enjoy them for what they are, a touch of fun in the kitchen, and hope that they also work well.

Left: Peeler with brush.

Above: Thick-grip peelers.

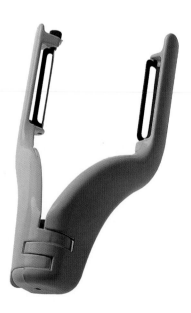

Above: Twin-bladed peeler.

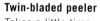

Above: Coloured peelers.

Above: A selection of graters, including single-sided, box and standard shapes.

Graters

The sturdier the better is the only approach if you want a grater for heavy-duty work, like grating large, raw potatoes. Standard or box graters are ideal and can have four or more sides with several different size blades, often including a slicer which acts like a mandoline. Some have simple removable base trays or come in their own box container, making it unnecessary to dirty a board or plate and leaving no messy trail. Single-sided graters can be difficult to hold unless you steady them with a damp cloth, but they are ideal to place over a bowl so that you can grate straight in. If you plan to put your grater in the dishwasher, look for a stainless steel one without too much plastic.

Paring Knives

These are one of the most important items in the kitchen, especially for small fiddly jobs. Choose a knife with a short enough blade to allow you to use your thumb as well, but not too short or you won't be able to use it for small chopping jobs. The knife should be curved but not serrated and it should have a sharp point. Don't be tempted by those with removable peeler blades, as these are easily lost and remove too much skin.

Above: Paring knives

Mandolines

The original mandoline was a simple wooden implement with adjustable flat or fluted blades. It was designed for chefs to cut wafer-thin slices of potato, or other hard foods like carrots, for making crisps (potato chips) and for shredding and chipping. Take care, as they can give your hands a nasty cut.

Modern mandolines These now often come in their own supporting plastic frame or box, sometimes with a shredder or chipper blade as well. They can have two or three blades which are adjustable to give variable thicknesses, and these are flat or fluted. Some of the plastic ones are machine washable and come with a gadget for holding the last part of the vegetable to protect you from slicing your fingertips.

For large quantities of chips (french fries) and crisps (chips) where the thickness needs to be exact, a more professional mandoline is available, but it is very expensive.

Left: Mandoline.

Wire Baskets

Using a wire basket is the easiest way to remove a batch of chips quickly from hot fat or quantities of potato from boiling water. When putting potatoes into hot fat do be sure the basket is heated in the fat first or the potatoes will stick to it.

Long-handled wire baskets

For blanching or deep-frying, these come in various sizes. Be sure to choose one that fits your pan almost exactly.
Small baskets Used for removing small quantities or pieces of potato when blanching or frying. There is a special attached pair for making potato nests.

Steamers

Steaming gives a very light potato and has nutritional benefits since it allows far fewer vitamins to be lost during cooking. Electric steamers are excellent for large quantities of potatoes. Chinese steamer baskets, which have their own lids,

are also good, especially as you can stack them up and steam several different foods at once. Clean steamers well to remove the potato starch – this is easiest done whilst they are warm.
Stainless steel steamer Can be bought with its matching pan, or separately to stand over a similar sized pan. It should

Above: Stainless steel steamer.

also have a lid which makes it very useful for keeping cooked potatoes warm until needed.
Collapsible steamer These will fit into most sizes of pan. Alternatively, use a colander with your own pan lid.

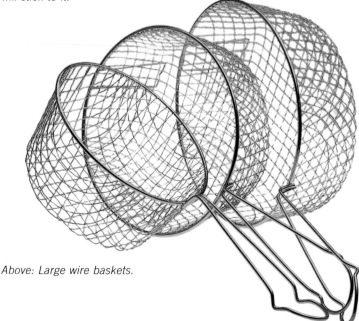

Above: Large wire baskets.

Above: Attached baskets.

Below: Metal ricer.

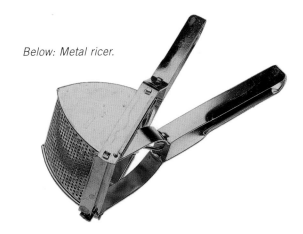

Below: Mouli grater.

Ricers and Mashers

A ricer is a small rigid sieve (strainer) with a pusher that makes the cooked potato come through looking like grains of rice. Potato was often served like this, riced directly into a warmed serving dish without any butter or milk added a much healthier version of mashed potatoes. It is also a very easy way to prepare mash so that it is ready to fork in the other ingredients. You can also use a basher or wooden implement to bash the potatoes around the pan in the old-fashioned way or just to help let off some steam.

Original metal ricer This has a triangular shaped bowl and is very sturdy. The round ricer doesn't take quite so much potato in the bowl.

Plastic ricer These are machine washable. They can have two sizes of blades, for smooth or textured results.

Mashers These come in various shapes and with different size holes, so you can choose accordingly if you prefer a smooth or rough mash. Some, but not all mashers, are machine washable.

Wooden basher A strong tool, which can give a chunky or fine result.

Large mouli grater This gives a very smooth result, and is suitable for puréeing or preparing a baby's dinner.

Left: Mashers.

Electrical Equipment

Food processor If you frequently slice, shred or make chips (french fries) then a processor with these attachments could be a great time-saver. Different models have different attachments so research well before you buy. Most will have one slicer and one shredder blade, some will have additional sizes of blades and shredders and some also have chipper attachments.

Potato peeler It only takes a few minutes to peel the potatoes, whilst you are doing other things. It does leave a slightly rough surface on the potatoes which is good for roasting, but don't put too many in the machine at one time.

Deep-fat Fryers

Making chips is one of the greatest causes of house fires so if you are a chip-loving family, it is essential that you buy an efficient deep-fat fryer (electric or not). Check the size before you buy as some can be quite small. Cooking chips in smaller quantities gives better results, and you should never be tempted to put in too many chips as the fat may bubble over. Don't buy a cheap fryer thinking it is saving you money because it won't last as long and will probably not be as safe. For the most efficient results be sure to keep the fryer well cleaned, change the oil frequently and preferably after each use. A good non-electric deep-fat fryer should be quite heavy, with a strong heatproof handle or handles and good-fitting basket and lid.

Electric deep-fat fryers

These have a thermostatically controlled temperature gauge so you fry at the right temperature, giving the crispest results. They often include specified temperature guides or controls for certain frying tasks. The fat and chips are in a sealed container which avoids smells and spitting fat and removes much of the danger. Most can be taken to pieces for easy cleaning or have removable electric cords and some have plastic lids so that you can see the food cooking.

Above: Deep-fat fryer.

Potato Bake Stands

To speed up baking you can push your potatoes on to skewers, or stand them upright on a special potato bake stand, which can save up to one-third of the cooking time.

Above: Food processor.

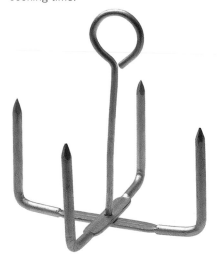

Above: Potato bake stand.

Chip Cutters

Manual chip cutters can certainly take the time out of chip making but you will always have to cut the potato to fit the model before you start cutting chips. It really would be good if you could try these out first though, as they rely entirely on brute force. Blades should be removable for easy washing and the rest of the machine should also be easily washable.

Flat chip cutter This gives very neat, if small, chips, but is hard work.

Upright chip cutter Slightly easier to push down, this cutter has two sizes of blade but is very limited on the size of potato it can take.

Above: Scrubbing brushes.

Above: Upright chip cutter.

Scrubbing brushes

For easily cleaning mud off potatoes, a small brush is ideal. The bristles should be firm without being too hard on the skins as you do not want to remove then while you are scrubbing.

Potato Pots

The two terracotta and clay pots illustrated are designed specifically for potatoes, giving an earthy taste and an easy method of cooking. Remember to soak the pots in water before using, as it is this moisture which is important in the cooking.

Potato Ballers

To make potato garnishes or shapes, the large side of a potato baller is ideal if you have a firm wrist.

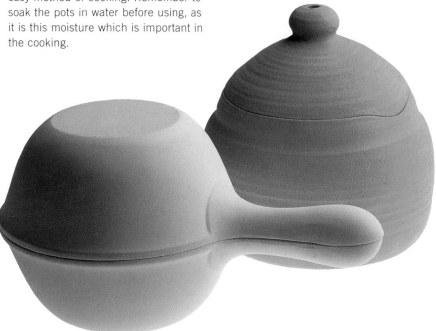

Right: Potato pots.

NEW POTATOES

The new potato heralds the beginning of the potato year. We call them new
or early potatoes as they are the first of that year's crop to be harvested.
After as little as 100 days underground certain potato varieties are
ready for picking, their skins still fragile and flaky and their flesh firm
and often quite crisp when lightly cooked.

The best new potatoes are quite delicious simply served with butter and fresh
herbs, but to the creative cook they are surprisingly flexible. When still firm,
almost crunchy, they are great in salads and their fresh earthy tastes can cope
with the strong tangy flavours of garlic sausage or Cajun spices. Firm, waxy new
potatoes are ideal to skewer and barbecue, or try serving them with the melting
Swiss cheese, raclette. And as they get bigger, towards the end of the new
season, they are great thickly sliced for casseroles and pies, perfect for roasting
whole with onions and herbs, and ideal layered into frittatas. Waxy potatoes are
also delicious in the Italian classic dish, gnocchi.

THE SIMPLEST POTATO SALAD

THE SECRET OF THIS POTATO SALAD IS TO MIX THE POTATOES WITH THE DRESSING WHILE THEY ARE STILL HOT SO THAT THEY ABSORB IT. THIS IS PERFECT WITH PAN-FRIED PORK, LAMB CHOPS OR ROAST CHICKEN. FOR VEGETARIANS, SERVE WITH A SELECTION OF ROASTED VEGETABLES.

SERVES FOUR TO SIX

INGREDIENTS
675g/1½lb small new or
  salad potatoes
4 spring onions (scallions)
45ml/3 tbsp olive oil
15ml/1 tbsp white wine vinegar
175ml/6fl oz/¾ cup good
  mayonnaise, preferably home-made
45ml/3 tbsp chopped chives
salt and ground black pepper

1 Cook the potatoes in their skins in a large pan of boiling salted water until tender.

2 Meanwhile, finely chop the white parts of the spring onions along with a little of the green parts; they look more attractive cut on the diagonal. Put to one side.

3 Whisk together the oil and vinegar. Drain the potatoes well and place them in a large bowl, then immediately toss lightly with the vinegar mixture and spring onions. Put the bowl to one side to cool.

4 Stir the mayonnaise and chives into the potatoes, season well and chill thoroughly until ready to serve. Adjust the seasoning before serving.

POTATO AND RADISH SALAD

RADISHES ADD A SPLASH OF CRUNCH AND PEPPERY FLAVOUR TO THIS HONEY-SCENTED SALAD. SO MANY POTATO SALADS ARE DRESSED IN A THICK SAUCE. THIS ONE, HOWEVER, IS QUITE LIGHT AND COLOURFUL WITH A TASTY YET DELICATE DRESSING.

SERVES FOUR TO SIX

INGREDIENTS
450g/1lb new or salad potatoes
45ml/3 tbsp olive oil
15ml/1 tbsp walnut or hazelnut oil
  (optional)
30ml/2 tbsp wine vinegar
10ml/2 tsp coarse-grain mustard
5ml/1 tsp honey
about 6–8 radishes, thinly sliced
30ml/2 tbsp chopped chives
salt and ground black pepper

VARIATIONS
Sliced celery, diced red onion and/or chopped walnuts would make good alternatives to the radishes if you can't get hold of any.

COOK'S TIP
For best effect, serve on a platter lined with frilly lettuce leaves.

1 Cook the potatoes in their skins in a large pan of boiling salted water until just tender. Drain the potatoes through a colander and leave to cool slightly. When cool enough to handle, cut the potatoes in half, but leave any small ones whole. Return the potatoes to a large bowl.

2 To make the dressing, place the oils, vinegar, mustard, honey and seasoning in a bowl. Mix them together until thoroughly combined.

3 Pour the dressing into the potatoes in the bowl while they are still cooling and toss. Leave to stand for an hour or so to allow the flavours to penetrate.

4 Finally mix in the sliced radishes and chopped chives and chill in the refrigerator until ready to serve.

5 When ready to serve, toss the salad mixture together again, as some of the dressing may have settled on the bottom, and adjust the seasoning.

TANGY POTATO SALAD

IF YOU LIKE A GOOD KICK OF MUSTARD, YOU'LL LOVE THIS COMBINATION. IT'S ALSO WELL FLAVOURED WITH TARRAGON, USED IN THE DRESSING AND AS A GARNISH.

SERVES EIGHT

INGREDIENTS

   1.3kg/3lb small new or salad
     potatoes
   30ml/2 tbsp white wine vinegar
   15ml/1 tbsp Dijon mustard
   45ml/3 tbsp vegetable or olive oil
   75g/3oz/6 tbsp chopped red onion
   125ml/4fl oz/½ cup mayonnaise
   30ml/2 tbsp chopped fresh tarragon,
     or 7.5ml/1½ tsp dried tarragon
   1 celery stick, thinly sliced
   salt and ground black pepper
   celery leaves and tarragon leaves,
     to garnish

VARIATIONS
When available, use small red or even blue potatoes to give a nice colour to the salad.

1 Cook the potatoes in their skins in boiling salted water for about 15–20 minutes until tender. Drain well.

2 Mix together the vinegar and mustard, then slowly whisk in the oil.

3 When the potatoes are cool enough to handle, slice them into a large bowl.

4 Add the onion to the potatoes and pour the dressing over them. Season, then toss gently to combine. Leave to stand for at least 30 minutes.

5 Mix together the mayonnaise and tarragon. Gently stir into the potatoes, along with the celery. Serve garnished with celery leaves and tarragon.

SAUSAGE AND POTATO SALAD

WELL-FLAVOURED SAUSAGES AND FIRM CHUNKY POTATOES MAKE A REALLY GREAT LUNCH,
SIMPLY DRESSED WITH A QUICK AND EASY VINAIGRETTE.

3 Peel the potatoes if you like or leave in their skins, and cut into 5mm/¼in slices. Place them in a large bowl and sprinkle with the wine and shallots.

4 To make the vinaigrette, mix together the mustard and vinegar in a small bowl, then very slowly whisk in the oil. Season and pour over the potatoes.

SERVES FOUR

INGREDIENTS
  450g/1lb small new or
    salad potatoes
  30–45ml/2–3 tbsp dry white wine
  2 shallots, finely chopped
  15ml/1 tbsp chopped fresh parsley
  15ml/1 tbsp chopped fresh tarragon
  175g/6oz cooked garlic or
    Toulouse sausage
  chopped fresh parsley, to garnish
For the vinaigrette
  10ml/2 tsp Dijon mustard
  15ml/1 tbsp tarragon vinegar or
    white wine vinegar
  75ml/5 tbsp extra virgin olive oil
  salt and ground black pepper

1 Cook the potatoes in their skins in a large pan of boiling salted water for 10–12 minutes until tender.

2 Drain the potatoes, rinse under cold running water, then drain them again.

5 Add the chopped herbs to the potatoes and toss until well mixed.

6 Slice the sausage and toss with the potatoes. Season to taste and serve at room temperature with a parsley garnish.

PERFECT CREAMED POTATOES

REAL CREAMED POTATOES ARE A SIMPLE LUXURY YOU WILL FIND IN ANY FASHIONABLE RESTAURANT TODAY BUT ARE SO EASY TO MAKE AT HOME AS WELL.

SERVES FOUR

INGREDIENTS

   900g/2lb small new potatoes,
    diced
   45ml/3 tbsp extra virgin olive oil
   about 150ml/¼ pint/⅔ cup hot milk
   freshly grated nutmeg
   a few fresh basil leaves or parsley
    sprigs, chopped
   salt and ground black pepper
   basil leaves, to garnish
   fried bacon, to serve

COOK'S TIP

Choosing the right potato makes all the difference to creamed ones. A waxy variety won't be light and fluffy, and a potato which breaks down too quickly on boiling will become a slurry.

1 Cook the potatoes in boiling water until just tender but not too mushy. Drain very well. Press the potatoes through a special potato "ricer" (rather like a large garlic press) or mash them well with a potato masher. Do not use a food processor as it can give the potatoes a gluey consistency.

2 Beat in olive oil and enough hot milk to make a smooth, thick purée.

3 Flavour to taste with the nutmeg and seasoning, then stir in the chopped fresh herbs. Spoon into a warm serving dish and serve at once, garnished with basil leaves and fried bacon.

POTATOES WITH RED CHILLIES

IF YOU LIKE CHILLIES, YOU'LL LOVE THESE POTATOES! IF YOU'RE NOT A FAN OF FIERY FLAVOURS, THEN SIMPLY LEAVE OUT THE CHILLI SEEDS AND USE THE FLESH BY ITSELF.

SERVES FOUR

INGREDIENTS

   12–14 small new or salad
    potatoes, halved
   30ml/2 tbsp vegetable oil
   2.5ml/½ tsp crushed dried
    red chillies
   2.5ml/½ tsp white cumin seeds
   2.5ml/½ tsp fennel seeds
   2.5ml/½ tsp crushed coriander
    seeds
   5ml/1 tsp salt
   1 onion, sliced
   1–4 fresh red chillies, chopped
   15ml/1 tbsp chopped fresh coriander
    (cilantro), plus extra to garnish

COOK'S TIP

To prepare fresh chillies, slit down one side and scrape out the seeds. Finely slice or chop the flesh. Wear rubber gloves if you have very sensitive skin.

1 Cook the potatoes in boiling salted water until tender but still firm. Remove from the heat and drain off the water. Set aside until needed.

2 In a deep frying pan, heat the oil over a medium-high heat, then reduce the heat to medium. Add the crushed chillies, cumin, fennel and coriander seeds and salt and fry, stirring, for 30–40 seconds.

3 Add the sliced onion and fry until golden brown. Then add the potatoes, red chillies and coriander and stir well.

4 Reduce the heat to very low, then cover and cook for 5–7 minutes. Serve the potatoes hot, garnished with more fresh coriander.

HOT HOT CAJUN POTATO SALAD

IN CAJUN COUNTRY WHERE TABASCO ORIGINATES, HOT MEANS REALLY HOT, SO YOU CAN GO TO TOWN WITH THIS SALAD IF YOU THINK YOU CAN TAKE IT!

SERVES SIX TO EIGHT

INGREDIENTS

18–24 waxy potatoes
1 green (bell) pepper, seeded
  and diced
1 large gherkin, chopped
4 spring onions (scallions), shredded
3 hard-boiled eggs, shelled
  and chopped
250ml/8fl oz/1 cup mayonnaise
15ml/1 tbsp Dijon mustard
a pinch or two of cayenne pepper
Tabasco sauce, to taste
salt and ground black pepper
sliced gherkin, to garnish
mayonnaise, to serve

3 In a separate bowl, mix the mayonnaise with the mustard and season with salt, black pepper and Tabasco sauce to taste.

4 Toss the dressing into the potato mixture and sprinkle with a pinch or two of cayenne. Serve with mayonnaise and a garnish of sliced gherkin.

1 Cook the potatoes in their skins in boiling salted water until tender. Drain and leave to cool. When they are cool enough to handle, peel them and cut into coarse chunks.

2 Place the potatoes in a large bowl and add the green pepper, gherkin, spring onions and hard-boiled eggs. Toss gently to combine.

POTATO GNOCCHI

GNOCCHI ARE LITTLE ITALIAN DUMPLINGS MADE EITHER WITH MASHED POTATO AND FLOUR, OR WITH SEMOLINA. TO ENSURE THAT THEY ARE LIGHT AND FLUFFY, TAKE CARE NOT TO OVERMIX THE DOUGH.

4 Divide the dough into 4 pieces. On a lightly floured surface, form each into a roll about 2cm/¾in in diameter. Cut the rolls crossways into pieces about 2cm/¾in long.

5 Hold an ordinary table fork with tines sideways, leaning on the board. Then one by one, press and roll the gnocchi lightly along the tines of the fork towards the points, making ridges on one side, and a depression from your thumb on the other.

6 Bring a large pan of salted water to a fast boil, then drop in about half the prepared gnocchi.

7 When the gnocchi rise to the surface, after 3–4 minutes, they are done. Lift them out with a slotted spoon, drain well, and place in a warmed serving bowl. Dot with butter. Cover to keep warm while cooking the remainder. As soon as they are cooked, toss the gnocchi with the butter, garnish with Parmesan shavings and fresh basil leaves, and serve immediately.

SERVES FOUR TO SIX

INGREDIENTS
 1kg/2¼lb waxy new potatoes
 250–300g/9–11oz/2¼–2¾ cups
  plain (all-purpose) flour, plus more
  if necessary
 1 egg
 pinch of freshly grated nutmeg
 25g/1oz/2 tbsp butter
 salt
 fresh basil leaves, to garnish
 Parmesan cheese cut in shavings,
  to garnish

COOK'S TIP
Gnocchi are also excellent served with a heated sauce, such as Bolognese.

1 Cook the potatoes in their skins in a large pan of boiling salted water until tender but not falling apart. Drain and peel while the potatoes are still hot.

2 Spread a layer of flour on a work surface. Pass the hot potatoes through a food mill, dropping them directly on to the flour. Sprinkle with about half of the remaining flour and mix in very lightly. Break the egg into the mixture.

3 Finally add the nutmeg to the dough and knead lightly, adding more flour if the mixture is too loose. When the dough is light to the touch and no longer moist it is ready to be rolled.

POTATOES <u>IN A</u> YOGURT SAUCE

TINY POTATOES WITH SKINS ON ARE DELICIOUS IN THIS FAIRLY SPICY YET TANGY YOGURT SAUCE.
SERVE WITH ANY MEAT OR FISH DISH OR JUST WITH HOT CHAPATIS.

SERVES FOUR

INGREDIENTS
    12 small new or salad
      potatoes, halved
    275g/10oz/1¼ cups natural (plain)
      low-fat yogurt
    300ml/½ pint/1¼ cups water
    1.5ml/¼ tsp turmeric
    5ml/1 tsp chilli powder
    5ml/1 tsp ground coriander
    2.5ml/½ tsp ground cumin
    5ml/1 tsp salt
    5ml/1 tsp soft brown sugar
    30ml/2 tbsp vegetable oil
    5ml/1 tsp white cumin seeds
    15ml/1 tbsp chopped fresh coriander
      (cilantro)
    2 fresh green chillies, sliced
    1 coriander sprig, to garnish

1 Cook the potatoes in their skins in boiling salted water until just tender, then drain and set aside.

2 Mix together the yogurt, water, turmeric, chilli powder, ground coriander, ground cumin, salt and sugar in a bowl. Set aside.

3 Heat the oil in a medium pan over a medium-high heat and stir in the white cumin seeds.

4 Reduce the heat to medium, and stir in the prepared yogurt mixture. Cook the sauce, stirring continuously, for about 3 minutes.

5 Add the fresh coriander, green chillies and potatoes to the sauce. Mix well and cook for 5–7 minutes, stirring occasionally.

6 Transfer to a serving dish, garnish with the coriander sprig, and serve hot.

COOK'S TIP
If new or salad potatoes are unavailable, use 450g/1lb ordinary potatoes instead, but not the floury type. Peel them and cut into large chunks, then cook as described above.

POTATOES, PEPPERS AND SHALLOTS ROASTED WITH ROSEMARY

THESE POTATOES SOAK UP BOTH THE TASTE AND WONDERFUL AROMAS OF THE SHALLOTS AND ROSEMARY — JUST WAIT TILL YOU OPEN THE OVEN DOOR.

SERVES FOUR

INGREDIENTS
500g/1¼lb waxy new potatoes
12 shallots
2 sweet yellow (bell) peppers
olive oil
2 rosemary sprigs
salt and ground black pepper
crushed peppercorns, to garnish

1 Preheat the oven to 200°C/400°F/ Gas 6. Par-boil the potatoes in their skins in boiling salted water for 5 minutes. Drain and when they are cool, peel them and halve lengthways.

COOK'S TIP
Liven up a simple dish of roast or grilled (broiled) lamb or chicken with these delicious and easy potatoes.

2 Peel the shallots, allowing them to fall into their natural segments. Cut each sweet pepper lengthways into eight strips, discarding seeds and pith.

3 Oil a shallow ovenproof dish thoroughly with olive oil. Arrange the potatoes and peppers in alternating rows and stud with the shallots.

4 Cut the rosemary sprigs into 5cm/2in lengths and tuck among the vegetables. Season the vegetables generously with salt and pepper, add the olive oil and roast, uncovered, for 30–40 minutes until all the vegetables are tender. Turn the vegetables occasionally to cook and brown evenly. Serve hot or at room temperature, with crushed peppercorns.

POTATOES WITH BLUE CHEESE AND WALNUTS

FIRM SMALL POTATOES, SERVED IN A CREAMY BLUE CHEESE SAUCE WITH THE CRUNCH OF WALNUTS, MAKE A GREAT SIDE DISH TO A SIMPLE ROAST MEAL. FOR A CHANGE, SERVE IT AS A LUNCH DISH OR A LIGHT SUPPER WITH A GREEN SALAD.

SERVES FOUR

INGREDIENTS
    450g/1lb small new or
      salad potatoes
    1 small head of celery, sliced
    1 small red onion, sliced
    115g/4oz/1 cup blue cheese, mashed
    150ml/¼ pint/⅔ cup single (light)
      cream
    50g/2oz/½ cup walnut pieces
    30ml/2 tbsp chopped fresh parsley
    salt and ground black pepper

COOK'S TIP
Use a combination of blue cheeses, such as Dolcelatte and Roquefort, or go for the distinctive flavour of Stilton on its own. If walnuts are not available, blue cheeses marry equally well with hazelnuts.

1 Cook the potatoes in their skins in a large pan with plenty of boiling water for about 15 minutes or until tender, adding the sliced celery and onion to the pan for the last 5 minutes or so of cooking.

2 Drain the vegetables well through a colander and put them into a shallow serving dish.

3 In a small pan, slowly melt the cheese in the cream, stirring occasionally. Do not allow the mixture to boil but heat it until it scalds.

4 Check the sauce and season to taste. Pour it evenly over the vegetables in the dish and sprinkle over the walnut pieces and fresh parsley. Serve hot, straight from the dish.

RACLETTE WITH NEW POTATOES

TRADITIONAL TO BOTH SWITZERLAND AND FRANCE, RACLETTE MELTS TO A VELVETY CREAMINESS AND WARM GOLDEN COLOUR AND HAS A SAVOURY TASTE WITH A HINT OF SWEETNESS.

SERVES FOUR

INGREDIENTS
For the relish
    2 red onions, sliced
    5ml/1 tsp sugar
    90ml/6 tbsp red wine vinegar
    2.5ml/½ tsp salt
    generous pinch of dried dill
For the potatoes
    500g/1¼lb new or salad potatoes,
      halved if large
    250g/9oz raclette cheese slices
    salt and ground black pepper

1 To make the relish, spread out the onions in a glass dish, pour over boiling water to cover and leave until cold.

2 Meanwhile mix the sugar, vinegar, salt and dill in a small pan. Heat gently, stirring, until the sugar has dissolved, then set aside to cool.

3 Drain the onions and return them to the dish, pour the vinegar mixture over, cover and leave for at least 1 hour, preferably overnight.

4 Cook the potatoes in their skins in boiling water until tender, then drain and place in a roasting pan. Preheat the grill (broiler). Season the potatoes and arrange the raclette on top. Place the pan under the grill until the cheese melts. Serve hot. Drain the excess vinegar from the red onion relish and serve with the potatoes.

COOK'S TIP
To speed up the process look for ready-sliced raclette for this dish. It is available from most large supermarkets and specialist cheese stores.

POTATO SKEWERS WITH MUSTARD DIP

POTATOES COOKED ON THE BARBECUE HAVE A GREAT FLAVOUR AND CRISP SKIN. TRY THESE DELICIOUS KEBABS SERVED WITH A THICK, GARLIC-RICH DIP.

SERVES FOUR

INGREDIENTS

For the dip
- 4 garlic cloves, crushed
- 2 egg yolks
- 30ml/2 tbsp lemon juice
- 300ml/½ pint/1¼ cups extra virgin olive oil
- 10ml/2 tsp whole-grain mustard
- salt and ground black pepper

For the skewers
- 1kg/2¼lb small new potatoes
- 200g/7oz shallots, halved
- 30ml/2 tbsp olive oil
- 15ml/1 tbsp sea salt

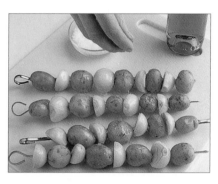

3 Par-boil the potatoes in their skins in boiling water for 5 minutes. Drain well and then thread them on to metal skewers alternating with the shallots.

4 Brush the skewers with oil and sprinkle with salt. Cook over a barbecue for 10–12 minutes, turning occasionally, Serve with the dip.

1 Prepare the barbecue for cooking the skewers before you begin. To make the dip, place the garlic, egg yolks and lemon juice in a blender or a food processor fitted with the metal blade and process for a few seconds until the mixture is smooth.

2 Keep the blender motor running and add the oil very gradually, pouring it in a thin stream, until the mixture forms a thick, glossy cream. Add the mustard and stir the ingredients together, then season with salt and pepper. Chill until ready to use.

COOK'S TIP
New potatoes and salad potatoes have a firmness necessary to stay on the skewer. Don't be tempted to use other types of small potato, they will probably split or fall off the skewers during cooking.

POTATO, MOZZARELLA AND GARLIC PIZZA

NEW POTATOES, SMOKED MOZZARELLA AND GARLIC MAKE THIS PIZZA UNIQUE. YOU COULD ADD SLICED SMOKED PORK SAUSAGE OR PASTRAMI TO MAKE IT EVEN MORE SUBSTANTIAL.

SERVES TWO TO THREE

INGREDIENTS

350g/12oz small new or
  salad potatoes
45ml/3 tbsp olive oil
2 garlic cloves, crushed
1 pizza base, 25–30cm/
  10–12 in diameter
1 red onion, thinly sliced
150g/5oz/1¼ cups smoked mozzarella
  cheese, grated
10ml/2 tsp chopped fresh rosemary
  or sage
salt and ground black pepper
30ml/2 tbsp freshly grated Parmesan
  cheese, to garnish

1 Preheat the oven to 220°C/425°F/Gas 7. Cook the potatoes in boiling salted water for 5 minutes. Drain well and leave to cool. Peel and slice thinly.

2 Heat 30ml/2 tbsp of the oil in a frying pan. Add the sliced potatoes and garlic and fry for 5–8 minutes, turning frequently, until tender.

3 Brush the pizza base with the remaining oil. Sprinkle the onion over, then arrange the potatoes on top.

4 Sprinkle over the mozzarella and rosemary or sage and plenty of black pepper. Bake for 15–20 minutes until golden. To serve, sprinkle with Parmesan and more black pepper.

WILD MUSHROOM GRATIN WITH BEAUFORT CHEESE, NEW POTATOES AND WALNUTS

THIS IS ONE OF THE SIMPLEST AND MOST DELICIOUS WAYS OF COOKING MUSHROOMS. SERVE THIS DISH AS THE SWISS DO, WITH NEW POTATOES AND GHERKINS.

SERVES FOUR

INGREDIENTS
> 900g/2lb small new or
>   salad potatoes
> 50g/2oz/4 tbsp unsalted (sweet)
>   butter or 60ml/4 tbsp olive oil
> 350g/12oz/5 cups assorted wild and
>   cultivated mushrooms, thinly sliced
> 175g/6oz Beaufort or Fontina cheese,
>   thinly sliced
> 50g/2oz/½ cup broken walnuts,
>   toasted
> salt and ground black pepper
> 12 gherkins and mixed green salad
>   leaves, to serve

1 Cook the potatoes in boiling salted water for 20 minutes until tender. Drain and return to the pan. Add a little butter or oil and cover to keep warm.

2 Heat the remaining butter or the oil in a frying pan over a medium-high heat. Add the mushrooms and fry until their juices appear, then increase the heat and fry until most of their juices have cooked away. Season.

3 Meanwhile preheat the grill (broiler). Arrange the cheese on top of the mushroom slices, place the pan under the grill and grill (broil) until bubbly and golden brown. Sprinkle the gratin with walnuts and serve at once with the buttered potatoes and sliced gherkins. Serve a side dish of mixed green salad to complete this meal.

BAKED MUSSELS AND POTATOES

THIS IMAGINATIVE BAKED CASSEROLE USES SOME OF THE BEST ITALIAN FLAVOURS — TOMATOES, GARLIC, BASIL AND, OF COURSE, PLUMP, JUICY MUSSELS.

SERVES TWO TO THREE

INGREDIENTS
750g/1¾lb large mussels, in
  their shells
225g/8oz small firm new potatoes
75ml/5 tbsp olive oil
2 garlic cloves, finely chopped
8 fresh basil leaves, torn into pieces
2 medium tomatoes, peeled and
  thinly sliced
45ml/3 tbsp breadcrumbs
ground black pepper
basil leaves, to garnish

1 Prepare the mussels for cooking by cutting off the "beards", then scrub and soak them in several changes of cold water. Discard any with broken shells or ones that are open.

2 Place the mussels with a cupful of water in a large pan over a medium heat. As soon as they open, lift them out. Remove and discard the empty half shells, leaving the mussels in the other half. (Discard any mussels that do not open at this stage.) Strain any cooking liquid remaining through a layer of kitchen paper, and reserve to add at the final stage.

3 Cook the potatoes in a large pan of boiling water until they are almost tender. Drain and leave to cool. When they are cool enough to handle, peel and slice them.

4 Preheat the oven to 180°C/350°F/Gas 4. Spread 30ml/2 tbsp of the olive oil in the bottom of a shallow ovenproof dish. Cover with the potato slices in one layer. Add the mussels in their half shells in one layer. Sprinkle with the garlic and basil. Cover with the tomato slices in one layer.

5 Sprinkle with breadcrumbs and black pepper, the reserved mussel cooking liquid and the remaining olive oil. Bake for about 20 minutes until the tomatoes are soft and the breadcrumbs are golden. Serve hot directly from the baking dish, and garnish with basil.

POTATO AND RED PEPPER FRITTATA

FRITTATA IS LIKE A LARGE OMELETTE. THIS TASTY VERSION IS FILLED WITH POTATOES AND PLENTY OF HERBS. DO USE FRESH MINT IN PREFERENCE TO DRIED IF YOU CAN FIND IT.

SERVES THREE TO FOUR

INGREDIENTS
450g/1lb small new or
  salad potatoes
6 eggs
30ml/2 tbsp chopped fresh mint
30ml/2 tbsp olive oil
1 onion, chopped
2 garlic cloves, crushed
2 red (bell) peppers, seeded and
  roughly chopped
salt and ground black pepper
mint sprigs, to garnish

1 Cook the potatoes in their skins in boiling salted water until just tender. Drain and leave to cool slightly, then cut into thick slices.

2 Whisk together the eggs, mint and seasoning in a bowl, then set aside. Heat the oil in a large frying pan.

3 Add the onion, garlic, peppers and potatoes to the pan and cook, stirring occasionally, for 5 minutes.

4 Pour the egg mixture over the vegetables in the frying pan and stir gently.

5 Push the mixture towards the centre of the pan as it cooks to allow the liquid egg to run on to the base. Meanwhile preheat the grill (broiler).

6 When the frittata is lightly set, place the pan under the hot grill for 2–3 minutes until the top is a light golden-brown colour.

7 Serve hot or cold, cut into wedges piled high on a serving dish and garnished with sprigs of mint.

TURKISH-STYLE NEW POTATO CASSEROLE

HERE'S A MEAL IN A POT THAT'S SUITABLE FOR FEEDING LARGE NUMBERS OF PEOPLE. IT'S LIGHTLY SPICED AND HAS PLENTY OF GARLIC — WHO COULD REFUSE?

SERVES FOUR

INGREDIENTS

60ml/4 tbsp olive oil
1 large onion, chopped
2 small–medium aubergines (eggplants), cut into small cubes
4 courgettes (zucchini), cut into small chunks
1 green (bell) pepper, seeded and chopped
1 red or yellow (bell) pepper, seeded and chopped
115g/4oz/1 cup fresh or frozen peas
115g/4oz green beans
450g/1lb new or salad potatoes, cubed
2.5ml/½ tsp cinnamon
2.5ml/½ tsp ground cumin
5ml/1 tsp paprika
4–5 tomatoes, skinned
400g/14oz can chopped tomatoes
30ml/2 tbsp chopped fresh parsley
3–4 garlic cloves, crushed
350ml/12fl oz/1½ cups vegetable stock
salt and ground black pepper
black olives and fresh parsley, to garnish

1 Preheat the oven to 190°C/375°F/ Gas 5. Heat 45ml/3 tbsp of the oil in a heavy pan, add the onion and fry until golden. Add the aubergines, sauté for about 3 minutes and then add the courgettes, green and red or yellow peppers, peas, beans and potatoes, together with the spices and seasoning.

2 Continue to cook for 3 minutes, stirring all the time. Transfer to a shallow ovenproof dish.

3 Halve, seed and chop the fresh tomatoes and mix with the canned tomatoes, parsley, garlic and the remaining olive oil in a bowl.

4 Pour the stock over the aubergine mixture and then spoon over the prepared tomato mixture.

5 Cover and bake the dish for 30–45 minutes until the vegetables are tender. Serve hot, garnished with black olives and parsley.

STEAK WITH STOUT AND POTATOES

THE IRISH WAY TO BRAISE BEEF IS IN STOUT, OF COURSE, AND TOPPED WITH THICKLY SLICED
POTATOES. BAKE IT IN A MODERATE OVEN FOR LONG, SLOW TENDERISING IF YOU PREFER.

SERVES FOUR

INGREDIENTS
    675g/1½lb stewing beef
    15ml/1 tbsp vegetable oil
    25g/1oz/2 tbsp butter
    225g/8oz tiny white onions
    175ml/6fl oz/¾ cup stout or dark beer
    300ml/½ pint/1¼ cups beef stock
    bouquet garni
    675g/1½lb firm, waxy new potatoes,
      cut into thick slices
    225g/8oz/3 cups large mushrooms,
      sliced
    15ml/1 tbsp plain (all-purpose) flour
    2.5ml/½ tsp mild mustard
    salt and ground black pepper
    chopped thyme sprigs, to garnish

3 Add the tiny white onions to the pan
and cook for 3–4 minutes until lightly
browned all over. Return the steak to
the pan with the onions. Pour on the
stout or beer and stock and season the
whole mixture to taste.

5 Add the sliced mushrooms over
the potatoes. Cover again and simmer
for a further 30 minutes or so.
Remove the steak and vegetables
with a slotted spoon and arrange on
a platter.

1 Trim any excess fat from the steak
and cut into four pieces. Season both
sides of the meat. Heat the oil and
10g/¼oz/1½ tsp of the butter in a large
heavy pan.

4 Next add the bouquet garni to the
pan and top with the potato slices
distributing them evenly over the
surface to cover the steak. Bring the
ingredients to a boil then reduce the
heat, cover with a tight-fitting lid and
simmer gently for 1 hour.

COOK'S TIP
To make onion peeling easier, first put
the onions in a bowl and cover with
boiling water. Allow them to soak for
about 5 minutes and drain. The skins
should now peel away easily.

6 Mix the remaining butter with the
flour to make a roux. Whisk a little at a
time into the cooking liquid in the pan.
Stir in the mustard. Cook over a
medium heat for 2–3 minutes, stirring
all the while, until thickened.

7 Season the sauce and pour over the
steak. Garnish with plenty of thyme
sprigs and serve the dish immediately.

VARIATION
For a dish that is lighter, but just as
tasty, substitute four lamb leg steaks for
the beef, and use dry (hard) cider
instead of the stout or beer, and lamb or
chicken stock instead of beef.

2 Add the steak and brown on both
sides, taking care not to burn the butter.
Remove from the pan and set aside.

SMOKED HADDOCK AND NEW POTATO PIE

SMOKED HADDOCK HAS A SALTY FLAVOUR AND CAN BE BOUGHT EITHER DYED OR UNDYED. THE DYED FISH HAS A STRONG YELLOW COLOUR WHILE THE OTHER IS ALMOST CREAMY IN COLOUR.

SERVES FOUR

INGREDIENTS
  450g/1lb smoked haddock
    fillet
  475ml/16fl oz/2 cups
    semi-skimmed (low-fat) milk
  2 bay leaves
  1 onion, quartered
  4 cloves
  450g/1lb new potatoes
  butter, for greasing
  30ml/2 tbsp cornflour
    (cornstarch)
  60ml/4 tbsp double (heavy) cream
  30ml/2 tbsp chopped fresh
    chervil
  salt and ground black pepper
  mixed vegetables, to serve

VARIATIONS
Instead of using all smoked haddock for this pie, use half smoked and half fresh. Cook the two types together, as described in Step 1. A generous handful of peeled prawns (shrimp) is also a good addition to this pie.

1 Preheat the oven to 200°C/400°F/Gas 6. Place the haddock in a deep-sided frying pan. Pour the milk over and add the bay leaves.

2 Stud the onion with the cloves and place it in the pan with the fish and milk. Cover the top and leave to simmer for about 10 minutes or until the fish starts to flake.

3 Remove the fish with a slotted spoon and set aside to cool. Strain the liquid from the pan into a separate pan and set aside.

4 To prepare the potatoes, cut them into fine slices, leaving the skins on.

5 Blanch the potatoes in a large pan of lightly salted water for 5 minutes. Drain.

6 Grease the base and sides of a 1.2 litre/2 pint/5 cup ovenproof dish. Then using a knife and fork, carefully flake the fish.

7 Reheat the milk in the pan. Mix the cornflour with a little water to form a paste and stir in the cream and the chervil. Add to the milk in the pan and cook until thickened.

8 Arrange one-third of the potatoes over the base of the dish and season with pepper. Lay half of the fish over. Repeat layering, finishing with a layer of potatoes on top.

9 Pour the sauce over the top, making sure that it sinks down through the mixture. Cover with foil and cook for 30 minutes. Remove the foil and cook for a further 10 minutes to brown the surface. Serve with a selection of mixed vegetables.

COOK'S TIP
The fish gives out liquid as it cooks, so it is best to start with a slightly thicker sauce than you might think is necessary.

MAINCROP POTATOES

As the season continues, the potatoes underground swell and firm up. The skin becomes thick enough to withstand storage through the long maincrop season and often well into the following year. Many maincrop potatoes have flesh that becomes soft and floury — a characteristic crucial for the perfect mash. They are used to make delicious soups, such as cream of cauliflower, or North African spiced soup, and are wonderful for creating fluffy, light fish pie toppings, and when added to dough to make delicious bread.

Maincrop potatoes can be fairly firm too and are suited to making the grated classic latkes, a Jewish potato pancake which needs to be fried until golden and crisp. Above all, maincrop potatoes are versatile — ideal for many dishes throughout their long season.

CHILLED LEEK AND POTATO SOUP

THIS CREAMY-SMOOTH COLD VERSION OF THE CLASSIC FRENCH SOUP VICHYSSOISE IS SERVED WITH THE REFRESHING TANG OF YOGURT AS A TOPPING.

SERVES FOUR

INGREDIENTS
    25g/1oz/2 tbsp butter
    15ml/1 tbsp vegetable oil
    1 small onion, chopped
    3 leeks, sliced
    2 medium floury potatoes, diced
    600ml/1 pint/2½ cups
      vegetable stock
    300ml/½ pint/1¼ cups milk
    45ml/3 tbsp single (light) cream
    a little extra milk (optional)
    salt and ground black pepper
    60ml/4 tbsp natural (plain) yogurt
      and fried chopped leeks, to serve

1 Heat the butter and oil in a large pan and add the onion, leeks and potatoes. Cover and cook for 15 minutes, stirring occasionally. Bring to the boil, reduce the heat and simmer for 10 minutes.

2 Stir in the stock and milk and cover again.

3 Ladle the vegetables and liquid into a blender or a food processor in batches and purée until smooth. Return to the pan, stir in the cream and season.

4 Leave the soup to cool, and then chill for 3–4 hours. You may need to add a little extra milk to thin down the soup, as it will thicken slightly as it cools.

5 Ladle the soup into soup bowls and serve topped with a spoonful of yogurt and a sprinkling of leeks.

POTATO LATKES

LATKES ARE TRADITIONAL JEWISH POTATO PANCAKES, FRIED UNTIL GOLDEN AND CRISP AND SERVED WITH HOT SALT BEEF OR APPLE SAUCE AND SOUR CREAM.

SERVES FOUR

INGREDIENTS
2 medium floury potatoes
1 onion
1 large egg, beaten
30ml/2 tbsp medium-ground
    matzo meal
vegetable oil, for frying
salt and ground black pepper

1 Coarsely grate the potatoes and the onion. Put them in a large colander but don't rinse them. Press them down, squeezing out as much of the thick starchy liquid as possible. Transfer the potato mixture to a bowl.

2 Immediately stir in the beaten egg. Add the matzo meal, stirring gently to mix. Season with salt and plenty of pepper.

VARIATION
Try using equal quantities of potatoes and Jerusalem artichokes for a really distinct flavour.

3 Heat a 1cm/½in layer of oil in a heavy frying pan for a few minutes (test it by throwing in a small piece of bread – it should sizzle). Take a spoonful of the potato mixture and lower it carefully into the oil. Continue adding spoonfuls, leaving space between each one.

4 Flatten the pancakes slightly with the back of a spoon. Fry for a few minutes until the latkes are golden brown on the underside, carefully turn them over and continue frying until golden brown.

5 Drain the latkes on kitchen paper, then transfer to an ovenproof serving dish and keep warm in a low oven while frying the remainder. Serve hot.

BIARRITZ POTATOES

A COMBINATION OF CLASSIC MASHED POTATOES WITH FINELY DICED HAM AND PEPPERS MIXED IN. THIS DISH IS GREAT SERVED WITH ROASTED CHICKEN.

SERVES FOUR

INGREDIENTS
900g/2lb floury potatoes
50g/2oz/4 tbsp butter
90ml/6 tbsp milk
50g/2oz cooked ham, finely diced
1 red (bell) pepper, deseeded and
    finely diced
15ml/1tbsp chopped fresh parsley
sea salt and ground black pepper

1 Peel and cut the potatoes into chunks. Boil in lightly salted water for 20 minutes or until very tender.

2 Drain and return the potatoes to the pan and allow the steam to dry off over a low heat.

3 Either mash or pass the potatoes through a potato ricer. Add the butter and milk and stir in the cooked ham, peppers and parsley. Season and serve.

LYONNAISE POTATOES

TWO SIMPLE INGREDIENTS ARE PREPARED SEPARATELY AND THEN TOSSED TOGETHER TO CREATE THE PERFECT COMBINATION. THESE POTATOES GO VERY WELL WITH A SIMPLE MEAT DISH, SUCH AS STEAK OR PORK CHOPS. SERVE WITH A BOWL OF GREEN BEANS, TOSSED IN BUTTER.

SERVES SIX

INGREDIENTS
900g/2lb floury potatoes
vegetable oil for shallow
    frying
25g/1oz/2 tbsp butter
15ml/1 tbsp olive oil
2 medium onions, sliced
    into rings
sea salt
15ml/1 tbsp chopped
    fresh parsley

VARIATION
For a more substantial version of this dish, ham or bacon can be added. Use about 50g/2oz chopped roast ham or bacon and fry with the onions until cooked through.

1 Scrub the potatoes clean and cook in a large pan with plenty of boiling water for 10 minutes.

2 Drain the potatoes through a colander and leave to cool slightly. When the potatoes are cool enough to handle, peel and finely slice them.

3 Heat the vegetable oil and shallow fry the potatoes in two batches for about 10 minutes until crisp, turning occasionally.

4 Meanwhile, melt the butter with the oil in a frying pan and fry the onions for 10 minutes until golden. Drain on kitchen paper.

5 Remove the potatoes with a slotted spoon and drain on kitchen paper. Toss with sea salt and carefully mix with the onions. Sprinkle with the parsley.

POTATO SKINS WITH CAJUN DIP

DIVINELY CRISP AND NAUGHTY, THESE POTATO SKINS ARE GREAT ON THEIR OWN OR SERVED WITH THIS PIQUANT DIP AS A GARNISH OR TO THE SIDE.

SERVES TWO

INGREDIENTS

    2 large baking potatoes
    vegetable oil, for deep frying
For the dip
    120ml/4fl oz/½ cup natural (plain)
      yogurt
    1 garlic clove, crushed
    5ml/1 tsp tomato purée (paste)
    2.5ml/½ tsp green chilli purée (paste)
      or ½ small green chilli, chopped
    1.5ml/¼ tsp celery salt
    salt and ground black pepper

COOK'S TIP
If you prefer, you can microwave the potatoes to save time. This will take about 10 minutes.

1 Preheat the oven to 180ºC/350ºF/Gas 4. Bake the potatoes for 45–50 minutes until tender. Cut them in half and scoop out the flesh, leaving a thin layer on the skins. Keep the flesh for another meal.

2 To make the dip, mix together all the ingredients and chill.

3 Heat a 1cm/½in layer of oil in a large pan or deep-fat fryer. Cut each potato half in half again, then fry them until crisp and golden on both sides. Drain on kitchen paper, sprinkle with salt and black pepper and serve with a bowl of dip or a dollop of dip in each skin.

POTATO PIZZA

THIS "PIZZA" MADE OF MASHED POTATOES, WITH A ROBUSTLY FLAVOURED FILLING OF ANCHOVIES,
CAPERS AND TOMATOES, IS A SPECIALITY OF PUGLIA IN NORTHERN ITALY.

SERVES FOUR

INGREDIENTS
1kg/2¼lb floury potatoes
120ml/4fl oz/½ cup extra virgin
  olive oil
2 garlic cloves, finely chopped
350g/12oz tomatoes, chopped
3 anchovy fillets, chopped
30ml/2 tbsp capers, rinsed
salt and ground black pepper

1 Cook the potatoes in their skins in boiling water until tender. Drain well and leave to cool slightly. When they are cool enough to handle, peel and mash or pass through a food mill. Beat in 45ml/3 tbsp of the oil and season to taste. Set aside.

2 Heat another 45ml/3 tbsp of the oil in a medium pan. Add the garlic and the chopped tomatoes and cook over a medium heat for 12–15 minutes stirring a little to cook evenly, until the tomatoes soften and begin to dry out. Meanwhile preheat the oven to 200°C/400°F/Gas 6.

3 Oil a round shallow baking dish. Spread half the mashed potatoes into the dish in an even layer. Cover with the tomatoes, and dot with the chopped anchovies and the capers.

4 Spread over the rest of the potatoes in an even layer. Brush the top with the remaining oil and bake for 20–25 minutes until the top is golden brown. Sprinkle with black pepper and serve hot.

VARIATION
For a vegetarian version of this dish, simply omit the anchovies. A few pitted and chopped olives may be added to the filling instead. Add them in step 3, on top of the tomatoes.

BAKED POTATOES AND THREE FILLINGS

POTATOES BAKED IN THEIR SKINS UNTIL THEY ARE CRISP ON THE OUTSIDE AND FLUFFY IN THE MIDDLE MAKE AN EXCELLENT AND NOURISHING MEAL ON THEIR OWN. BUT FOR AN EVEN BETTER TREAT, ADD ONE OF THESE DELICIOUS AND EASY TOPPINGS.

SERVES FOUR

INGREDIENTS
4 medium baking potatoes
olive oil
sea salt
filling of your choice (see below)

COOK'S TIP
Choose potatoes which are evenly sized and have undamaged skins, and scrub them thoroughly. If they are done before you are ready to serve them, take them out of the oven and wrap them up in a warmed cloth until they are needed.

1 Preheat the oven to 200ºC/400ºF/ Gas 6. Score the potatoes with a cross and rub all over with the olive oil.

2 Place on a baking sheet and cook for 45 minutes to 1 hour until a knife inserted into the centres indicates they are cooked. Or cook in the microwave according to your manufacturer's instructions.

3 Cut the potatoes open along the score lines and push up the flesh. Season and fill with your chosen filling.

STIR-FRY VEGETABLES
45ml/3 tbsp sunflower oil
2 leeks, thinly sliced
2 carrots, cut into sticks
1 courgette (zucchini), thinly sliced
115g/4oz baby corn, halved
115g/4oz/1½ cup button (white) mushrooms, sliced
45ml/3 tbsp soy sauce
30ml/2 tbsp dry sherry or vermouth
15ml/1 tbsp sesame oil
sesame seeds, to garnish

1 Heat the sunflower oil in a wok or large frying pan until really hot. Add the leeks, carrots, courgette and baby corn and stir-fry together for about 2 minutes, then add the mushrooms and stir-fry for a further minute. Mix the soy sauce, sherry or vermouth and sesame oil and pour over the vegetables. Heat through until just bubbling and scatter the sesame seeds over.

RED BEAN CHILLI
425g/15oz can red kidney beans, drained
200g/7oz/scant 1 cup low-fat cottage or cream cheese
30ml/2 tbsp mild chilli sauce
5ml/1 tsp ground cumin

1 Heat the beans in a pan or microwave and stir in the cottage or cream cheese, chilli sauce and cumin.

2 Serve topped with more chilli sauce.

CHEESE AND CREAMY CORN
425g/15oz can creamed corn
115g/4oz/1 cup hard cheese, grated
5ml/1 tsp mixed dried herbs
fresh parsley sprigs, to garnish

1 Heat the corn gently with the cheese and mixed herbs until well blended.

2 Use to fill the potatoes and garnish with fresh parsley sprigs.

POTATO BREAD <u>WITH</u> CARAMELIZED ONIONS <u>AND</u> ROSEMARY

THE ROSEMARY AND ONIONS INCORPORATED INTO THIS BREAD GIVE IT A MEDITERRANEAN FEEL. IT IS DELICIOUS SERVED WARM WITH A SIMPLE VEGETABLE SOUP.

MAKES A 900G/2LB LOAF

INGREDIENTS
    450g/1lb/4 cups strong white flour
    5ml/1 tsp easy-blend (rapid-rise)
      dried yeast
    a pinch of salt
    15g/½oz/1 tbsp butter
    325ml/11fl oz/1⅓ cups warmed milk
    15ml/1 tbsp olive oil
    2 medium onions, sliced into rings
    115g/4oz maincrop potatoes, grated
    1 sprig rosemary, chopped
    2.5ml/½ tsp sea salt

1 Sift the flour into a large bowl. Make a well in the centre and stir in the yeast and a pinch of salt. Rub in the butter until the mixture resembles fine breadcrumbs and then gradually pour in the lukewarm milk.

2 Stir the mixture with a round-bladed knife and then once the wet ingredients have become incorporated, bring it together with your fingers.

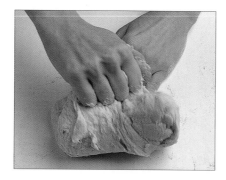

3 Turn the dough out and knead on a surface dusted with flour for 5 minutes or until the dough is smooth and elastic. Return the bread to a clean bowl and cover with a damp cloth. Leave to rise in a warm place for 45 minutes or until the dough has doubled in size.

4 Meanwhile, heat the oil in a pan and add the onions, stir over a low heat and cook for about 20 minutes until the onions are golden brown and very soft. Then set aside.

5 Bring a pan of lightly salted water to the boil and add the grated potatoes to the water. Cook for 5 minutes or until just tender. Drain and plunge into cold water.

VARIATION
For a more piquant flavour, add some bottled sundried tomatoes, drained of their oil and chopped, and a sprinkling of pitted black olives to the onion layers. Try fresh thyme for a subtle herby tang.

6 Turn the dough out of the bowl and knock back. Roll out on a lightly floured surface. Drain the potatoes and sprinkle half over the surface with a little rosemary and half the onions. Carefully roll the dough up into a sausage shape.

7 Lift the dough into an oiled 23 x 23cm/9 x 9in tin (pan). Using the palms of your hands flatten the dough out, making sure that the dough fits the tin neatly. Sprinkle the remaining potatoes and onions over the top with the sea salt and rosemary.

8 Cover again with a damp cloth and leave to rise for 20 minutes.

9 Meanwhile, preheat the oven to 220°C/425°F/Gas 7. Bake the bread for 15–20 minutes. Serve warm drizzled with a little extra olive oil if you like.

COOK'S TIP
If you don't like your onions very crisp, cover the loaf with foil after 10 minutes to prevent the surface from over-browning. Use the largest grater setting available on the food processor for the potatoes, to keep them from becoming too sticky when blanched.

MARQUIS POTATOES

A VARIATION ON THE DUCHESSE MIXTURE, FINISHED WITH A DELICIOUSLY TANGY TOMATO MIXTURE SET IN THE CENTRE OF THE POTATO NEST.

SERVES SIX

INGREDIENTS
  900g/2lb floury potatoes
  450g/1lb ripe tomatoes
  15ml/1tbsp olive oil
  2 shallots, finely chopped
  25g/1oz/2 tbsp butter
  3 egg yolks
  60ml/4 tbsp milk
  chopped fresh parsley, to garnish
  sea salt and ground black pepper

1 Peel the potatoes, cut them into small chunks, and boil in lightly salted water for 20 minutes or until very tender. Meanwhile, blanch the tomatoes in boiling water and then plunge into a bowl of cold water. Peel the skins and then scoop the seeds out. Chop the tomato flesh.

2 Heat the olive oil in a large frying pan and fry the shallots for 2 minutes stirring continuously. Add the chopped tomatoes to the pan and fry for a further 10 minutes until the moisture has evaporated. Set aside.

3 Drain the potatoes through a colander and return to the pan and allow the steam to dry off. Cool slightly and mash well with the butter and 2 of the egg yolks and the milk. Season with salt and ground black pepper.

4 Grease a baking sheet. Spoon the potato into a piping bag fitted with a medium star nozzle. Pipe six oval nests onto the baking sheet. Beat the remaining egg with a little water and carefully brush over the potato. Grill for 5 minutes or until golden.

5 Spoon the tomato mixture inside the nests and top with a little parsley and black pepper. Serve them immediately.

SARDINE AND LEEK POTATO CAKES

THIS IS A SIMPLE SUPPER USING A SELECTION OF BASIC STORE-CUPBOARD INGREDIENTS. USING SARDINES IN TOMATO SAUCE GIVES A GREATER DEPTH OF FLAVOUR TO THE FINISHED DISH.

SERVES SIX

INGREDIENTS
225g/8oz potatoes, diced
425g/15oz can sardines in tomato
  sauce, boned and flaked
1 small leek, very finely diced
5ml/1 tsp lemon juice
salt and ground black pepper
For the coating
1 egg, beaten
75g/3oz/1½ cups fresh white
  breadcrumbs
vegetable oil for frying
salad leaves, cucumber and lemon
  wedges, to garnish
mayonnaise, to serve
bread rolls, to serve (optional)

1 Cook the potatoes in lightly salted boiling water for 10 minutes or until tender. Drain, mash, and cool.

2 Add the sardines and their tomato sauce, leeks and lemon juice. Season with salt and pepper and then beat well until you have formed a smooth paste. Chill for 30 minutes.

3 Divide the mixture into six pieces and shape into cakes. Dip each cake in the egg and then the breadcrumbs.

4 Heat the oil and shallow-fry the fish cakes on each side for 5 minutes. Drain on kitchen paper and garnish with salad leaves, cucumber ribbons and lemon wedges. Serve with mayonnaise.

BUBBLE AND SQUEAK

WHETHER YOU HAVE LEFTOVERS, OR COOK THIS OLD-FASHIONED CLASSIC FROM FRESH, BE SURE TO GIVE IT A REALLY GOOD "SQUEAK" (FRY) IN THE PAN SO IT TURNS A RICH HONEY BROWN AS ALL THE FLAVOURS CARAMELIZE TOGETHER. IT IS KNOWN AS COLCANNON IN IRELAND, WHERE IT IS TURNED IN CHUNKS OR SECTIONS, PRODUCING A CREAMY BROWN AND WHITE CAKE.

3 Add the vegetables to the pan with the cooked onions, stir well, then press the vegetable mixture into a large, even cake.

4 Cook over a medium heat for about 15 minutes until the cake is browned underneath.

5 Invert a large plate over the pan, and, holding it tightly against the pan, turn them both over together. Lift off the frying pan, return it to the heat and add the remaining fat or oil. When hot, slide the cake back into the pan, browned side uppermost.

6 Cook over a medium heat for 10 minutes or until the underside is golden brown. Serve hot, in wedges.

COOK'S TIP
If you don't have leftover cooked cabbage or Brussels sprouts, shred raw cabbage and cook both in boiling salted water until tender. Drain, then chop.

SERVES FOUR

INGREDIENTS
  60ml/4 tbsp bacon fat or vegetable
    oil
  1 onion, finely chopped
  450g/1lb floury potatoes, cooked
    and mashed
  225g/8oz cooked cabbage or Brussels
    sprouts, finely chopped
  salt and ground black pepper

1 Heat 30ml/2 tbsp of the fat or oil in a heavy frying pan. Add the onion and cook, stirring frequently, until softened but not browned.

2 In a large bowl, mix together the potatoes and cooked cabbage or sprouts and season with salt and plenty of pepper to taste.

BAKED SCALLOPED POTATOES <u>WITH</u> FETA CHEESE <u>AND</u> OLIVES

THINLY SLICED POTATOES ARE COOKED WITH GREEK FETA CHEESE AND BLACK AND GREEN OLIVES IN OLIVE OIL. THIS DISH IS A GOOD ONE TO SERVE WITH TOASTED PITTA BREAD.

SERVES FOUR

INGREDIENTS
    900g/2lb maincrop potatoes
    150ml/¼ pint/⅔ cup olive oil
    1 sprig rosemary
    275g/10oz/2½ cups feta cheese,
      crumbled
    115g/4oz/1 cup pitted black and
      green olives
    300ml/½ pint/1¼ cups hot
      vegetable stock
    salt and ground black pepper

COOK'S TIP
Make sure you choose Greek feta cheese, which has a completely different texture to Danish.

1 Preheat the oven to 200°C/400°F/ Gas 6. Cook the potatoes in plenty of boiling water for 15 minutes. Drain and cool slightly. Peel the potatoes and cut into thin slices.

2 Brush the base and sides of a 1.5 litre/2½ pint/6¼ cup rectangular ovenproof dish with some of the olive oil.

3 Layer the potatoes in the dish with the rosemary, cheese and olives. Drizzle with the remaining olive oil and pour over the stock. Season the whole with salt and plenty of ground black pepper.

4 Cook for 35 minutes, covering with foil to prevent the potatoes from getting too brown. Serve hot, straight from the dish.

BERRICHONNE POTATOES

A POTATO DISH WITH A DIFFERENCE. THE TOP OF THE POTATOES WILL BE CRISPY WITH A SOFTLY COOKED BASE IN THE STOCK, ONIONS AND BACON.

SERVES FOUR

INGREDIENTS

    900g/2 lb maincrop potatoes
    25g/1oz/2 tbsp butter
    1 onion, finely chopped
    115g/4oz unsmoked streaky (fatty)
      bacon, rinds removed
    350ml/12fl oz/1½ cups
      vegetable stock
    chopped parsley, to garnish
    sea salt and ground black pepper

1   Preheat the oven to 200ºC/400ºF/ Gas 6. Peel the potatoes and trim them into barrel shapes. Leave the potatoes to stand in a bowl of cold water.

2   Melt the butter in a frying pan. Add the onions, stir and cover with a lid. Cook for 2–3 minutes, until they are soft but not brown.

3   Chop the bacon and add to the onions, cover and cook for 2 minutes.

4   Spoon the onion mixture into the base of a 1.5 litres/2½ pints/6¼ cups rectangular shallow ovenproof dish. Lay the potatoes over the onion mixture and pour the stock over, making sure that it comes halfway up the sides of them. Season and cook for 1 hour. Garnish with chopped parsley.

POLPETTES

Yummy little fried mouthfuls of potato and tangy-sharp Greek feta cheese, flavoured with dill and lemon juice. Serve as an appetizer or party bite.

SERVES FOUR

INGREDIENTS
  500g/1¼lb floury potatoes
  115g/4oz/1 cup feta cheese
  4 spring onions (scallions), chopped
  45ml/3 tbsp chopped fresh dill
  1 egg, beaten
  15ml/1 tbsp lemon juice
  plain (all-purpose) flour, for dredging
  45ml/3 tbsp olive oil
  salt and ground black pepper
  shredded spring onions and dill
    sprigs, to garnish
  lemon wedges, to serve

1 Cook the potatoes in their skins in boiling lightly salted water until soft. Drain and leave to cool slightly, then chop them in half and peel while still warm.

2 Place in a bowl and mash. Crumble the feta cheese into the potatoes and add the spring onions, dill, egg and lemon juice and season with salt and pepper. (The cheese is salty, so taste before you add salt.) Stir well.

3 Cover and chill until firm. Divide the mixture into walnut-size balls, then flatten them slightly. Dredge with flour, shaking off the excess.

4 Heat the oil in a frying pan and fry the polpettes in batches until golden brown on both sides. Drain on kitchen paper and serve hot, garnished with spring onions, dill and lemon wedges.

POTATO, BEEF, BEETROOT AND MUSHROOM GRATIN

THIS VARIATION OF AN UNUSUAL POLISH MIX OF FLAVOURS PRODUCES A VERY HEARTY MAIN MEAL. HORSERADISH AND MUSTARD ARE GREAT WITH BOTH THE BEEF AND THE BEETROOT, MOST OF WHICH IS HIDDEN UNDERNEATH MAKING A COLOURFUL SURPRISE WHEN YOU SERVE IT.

SERVES FOUR

INGREDIENTS
   30ml/2 tbsp vegetable oil
   1 small onion, chopped
   15ml/1 tbsp plain (all-purpose) flour
   150ml/¼ pint/⅔ cup vegetable stock
   225g/8oz cooked beetroot (beets),
      drained well and chopped
   15ml/1 tbsp creamed horseradish
   15ml/1 tbsp caraway seeds
   3 shallots, or 1 medium
      onion, chopped
   450g/1lb frying or grilling (broiling)
      steak, cut into thin strips
   225g/8oz assorted wild or cultivated
      mushrooms, sliced
   10–15ml/2–3 tsp hot mustard
   60ml/4 tbsp sour cream
   45ml/3 tbsp chopped fresh parsley
For the potato border
   900g/2lb floury potatoes
   150ml/¼ pint/⅔ cup milk
   25g/1oz/2 tbsp butter or margarine
   15ml/1 tbsp chopped fresh dill
      (optional)
   salt and ground black pepper

2 Return to the heat and simmer until thickened, stirring all the while. Add the beetroot (reserve a few pieces for the topping, if you wish), horseradish and caraway seeds. Mix gently, then put to one side.

3 To make the potato border, first cook the potatoes in a large pan with plenty of boiling salted water for 20 minutes until tender. Drain well through a colander and mash with the milk and butter or margarine. Add the chopped dill, if using, and season the mixture with salt and pepper to taste. Stir to combine the seasonings.

COOK'S TIP
If planning ahead, for instance for a dinner party, this entire dish can be made in advance and heated through when needed. Allow 50 minutes baking time from room temperature. Add the beetroot (beet) pieces to the topping near the end of the cooking time.

4 Spoon the potatoes into the prepared dish and push well up the sides, making a large hollow in the middle for the filling. Spoon the beetroot mixture into the well, evening it out with the back of a spoon, and set aside.

5 Heat the remaining oil in a large frying pan, add the shallots or onion and fry until softened but not coloured. Add the steak and stir-fry quickly until browned all over. Then add the mushrooms and fry quickly until most of their juices have cooked away. Remove the pan from the heat and gently stir in the mustard, sour cream, seasoning to taste and half the parsley until well blended.

6 Spoon the steak mixture over the beetroot mixture in the baking dish, sprinkling the reserved beetroot over the top, cover and bake for 30 minutes. Serve hot, straight from the dish, sprinkled with the remaining parsley.

1 Preheat the oven to 190°C/375°F/ Gas 5. Lightly oil a baking or gratin dish. Heat 15ml/1 tbsp of the oil in a large pan, add the onion and fry until softened but not coloured. Stir in the flour, remove from the heat and gradually add the stock, stirring until well blended and smooth.

LAMB PIE WITH MUSTARD THATCH

TRADITIONAL SHEPHERD'S PIE WITH A TWIST, THE MUSTARD GIVING A REAL TANG TO THE TOPPING.

2 Fry the lamb in a non-stick pan, breaking it up with a fork, until lightly browned all over. Add the onion, celery and carrots to the pan and cook for 2–3 minutes, stirring, to stop the mixture sticking to the pan.

3 Stir in the stock and cornflour mixture. Bring to the boil, stirring all the while, then remove from the heat. Stir in the Worcestershire sauce and rosemary and season with salt and pepper to taste.

4 Turn the lamb mixture into a 1.75 litre/3 pint/7 cup ovenproof dish and spread over the potato topping evenly, swirling with the edge of a palette knife to make an attractive pattern. Bake for 30–35 minutes until golden on the top. Serve hot.

VARIATION
Although the original shepherd's pie is made with lamb, most people make it with minced (ground) beef as well. To vary the topping slightly, try adding horseradish – either creamed or, for an even stronger flavour, freshly grated.

SERVES FOUR

INGREDIENTS
 800g/1¾lb floury potatoes, diced
 60ml/4 tbsp milk
 15ml/1 tbsp wholegrain or
  French mustard
 a little butter
 450g/1lb lean lamb, minced (ground)
 1 onion, chopped
 2 celery sticks, thinly sliced
 2 carrots, diced
 30ml/2 tbsp cornflour (cornstarch)
  blended into 150ml/¼ pint/⅔ cup
  lamb stock
 15ml/1 tbsp Worcestershire sauce
 30ml/2 tbsp chopped fresh rosemary
 salt and ground black pepper

1 Cook the potatoes in a large pan of boiling lightly salted water until tender. Drain well and mash until smooth, then stir in the milk, mustard, butter and seasoning to taste. Meanwhile preheat the oven to 200°C/400°F/Gas 6.

STOVED CHICKEN

"STOVIES" WERE ORIGINALLY — NOT SURPRISINGLY — POTATOES SLOWLY COOKED ON THE STOVE WITH ONIONS AND LARD OR BUTTER UNTIL FALLING TO PIECES. THIS VERSION INCLUDES A DELICIOUS LAYER OF BACON AND CHICKEN HIDDEN IN THE MIDDLE OF THE VEGETABLES.

SERVES FOUR

INGREDIENTS
  butter, for greasing
  1kg/2¼lb baking potatoes, cut into
    5mm/¼in slices
  2 large onions, thinly sliced
  15ml/1 tbsp chopped fresh thyme
  25g/1oz/2 tbsp butter
  15ml/1 tbsp vegetable oil
  2 large bacon slices, chopped
  4 large chicken joints, halved
  600ml/1 pint/2½ cups chicken stock
  1 bay leaf
  salt and ground black pepper

COOK'S TIP
Instead of chicken joints, choose eight chicken thighs or chicken drumsticks.

1 Preheat the oven to 150°C/300°F/ Gas 2. Arrange a thick layer of half the potato slices in the bottom of a large lightly greased heavy casserole, then cover with half the onions. Sprinkle with half of the thyme, and season with salt and pepper to taste.

2 Heat the butter and oil in a large heavy frying pan, add the bacon and chicken, stirring frequently, and brown on all sides. Using a slotted spoon, transfer the chicken and bacon to the casserole. Reserve the fat in the pan.

3 Sprinkle the remaining thyme over the chicken, season with salt and pepper, then cover with the remaining onion slices, followed by a neat layer of overlapping potato slices. Season the dish well.

4 Pour the stock into the casserole, add the bay leaf and brush the potatoes with the reserved fat. Cover tightly and bake for about 2 hours until the chicken is very tender.

5 Preheat the grill (broiler). Take the cover off the casserole and place it under the grill until the slices of potato are beginning to turn golden brown and crisp. Remove the bay leaf and serve hot.

COD, BASIL, TOMATO AND POTATO PIE

NATURAL AND SMOKED FISH MAKE A GREAT COMBINATION, ESPECIALLY WITH THE HINT OF TOMATO AND BASIL. SERVED WITH A GREEN SALAD, IT MAKES AN IDEAL DISH FOR LUNCH OR A FAMILY SUPPER.

2 Melt 75g/3oz/6 tbsp of the butter in a large pan, add the onion and cook for about 5 minutes until softened and tender but not browned. Sprinkle over the flour and half the chopped basil. Gradually add the reserved fish cooking liquid, adding a little more milk if necessary to make a fairly thin sauce, stirring constantly to make a smooth consistency. Bring to the boil, season with salt and pepper, and add the lemon thyme with the remaining basil.

3 Remove the pan from the heat, then add the fish and tomatoes and stir gently to combine. Pour into an ovenproof dish.

SERVES EIGHT

INGREDIENTS
    1kg/2¼lb smoked cod
    1kg/2¼lb white cod
    900ml/1½ pint/3¾ cups milk
    1.2 litres/2 pints/5 cups water
    2 basil sprigs
    1 lemon thyme sprig
    150g/5oz/10 tbsp butter
    1 onion, chopped
    75g/3oz/⅔ cup plain (all-purpose)
      flour
    30ml/2 tbsp chopped fresh basil
    4 firm plum tomatoes, peeled
      and chopped
    12 medium maincrop floury potatoes
    salt and ground black pepper
    crushed black peppercorns,
      to garnish
    green salad, to serve

1 Place both kinds of fish in a roasting pan with 600ml/1 pint/2½ cups of the milk, the water and the herb sprigs. Bring to a simmer and cook gently for about 3–4 minutes. Leave the fish to cool in the liquid for about 20 minutes. Drain the fish, reserving the cooking liquid for use in the sauce. Flake the fish, removing any skin and bone.

4 Preheat the oven to 180°C/350°F/ Gas 4. Cook the potatoes in boiling water until tender. Drain, then add the remaining butter and milk, and mash. Season to taste and spoon over the fish mixture, using a fork to create a pattern. You can freeze the pie at this stage. Bake for 30 minutes until the top is golden. Sprinkle with the crushed peppercorns and serve hot with salad.

CLASSIC FISH PIE

ORIGINALLY A FISH PIE WAS BASED ON THE "CATCH OF THE DAY". NOW WE CAN CHOOSE EITHER THE FISH WE LIKE BEST, OR THE VARIETY THAT OFFERS BEST VALUE FOR MONEY.

SERVES FOUR

INGREDIENTS
   butter, for greasing
   450g/1lb mixed fish, such as
      cod or salmon fillets and
      peeled prawns (shrimp)
   finely grated rind of 1 lemon
   450g/1lb floury potatoes
   25g/1oz/2 tbsp butter
   salt and ground black pepper
   1 egg, beaten
For the sauce
   15g/½oz/1 tbsp butter
   15ml/1 tbsp plain (all-purpose) flour
   150ml/¼ pint/⅔ cup milk
   45ml/3 tbsp chopped fresh parsley

1 Preheat the oven to 220°C/425°F/ Gas 7. Grease an ovenproof dish and set aside. Cut the fish into bitesize pieces. Season the fish, sprinkle over the lemon rind and place in the base of the prepared dish. Allow to sit while you make the topping.

2 Cook the potatoes in boiling salted water until tender.

3 Meanwhile make the sauce. Melt the butter in a pan, add the flour and cook, stirring, for a few minutes. Remove from the heat and gradually whisk in the milk. Return to the heat and bring to the boil then reduce the heat and simmer, whisking all the time, until the sauce has thickened and achieved a smooth consistency. Add the parsley and season to taste. Pour over the fish mixture.

4 Drain the potatoes well and then mash with the butter.

5 Pipe or spoon the potatoes on top of the fish mixture. Brush the beaten egg over the potatoes. Bake for 45 minutes until the top is golden brown. Serve hot.

COOK'S TIP
If using frozen fish defrost it very well first, as lots of water will ruin your pie.

SWEET POTATOES

Although no relation to the potato, the sweet potato cooks in exactly the same way and has all the same characteristics, however, the time it takes to cook is often lengthier. The two main varieties of sweet potato are both a recognizable yellowish orange colour.

The flesh of sweet potatoes has a soft texture that can be cooked in numerous ways. In hotter countries, where sweet potatoes originated, they are frequently served with lightly spiced foods. They are often found in fish dishes, such as sweet potato fish rolls, and also partner strong savoury flavours such as bacon. The traditional American dish, orange candied sweet potatoes, is flavoured with maple syrup and spices, and served with turkey at Thanksgiving.

The very name of the vegetable hints at a sweetness that inclines cooks to use sweet potatoes in baking too. Sweet potatoes are delicious in bread rolls and also taste superb as sweet potato muffins with raisins.

CORN AND SWEET POTATO SOUP

THE COMBINATION OF CORN AND SWEET POTATO GIVES THIS SOUP A REAL DEPTH OF FLAVOUR AS WELL AS MAKING IT LOOK VERY COLOURFUL.

SERVES SIX

INGREDIENTS

    15ml/1 tbsp olive oil
    1 onion, finely chopped
    2 garlic cloves, crushed
    1 small red chilli, seeded and
      finely chopped
    1.75 litres/3 pints/7½ cups
      vegetable stock
    10ml/2 tsp ground cumin
    1 medium sweet potato, diced
    ½ red (bell) pepper, finely
      chopped
    450g/1lb corn kernels
    salt and ground black pepper
    lime wedges, to serve

1 Heat the oil and fry the onion for 5 minutes until softened. Add the garlic and chilli and fry for a further 2 minutes.

2 In the same pan, add 300ml/½ pint/ 1¼ cups of the stock, and simmer for 10 minutes.

3 Mix the cumin with a little stock to form a paste, then stir into the soup.

4 Add the diced sweet potato, stir and then simmer for 10 minutes. Season and stir again.

5 Add the pepper, corn and remaining stock and simmer for 10 minutes. Process half of the soup until smooth and then stir into the chunky soup. Season and serve with lime wedges for squeezing over.

GLAZED SWEET POTATOES WITH BACON

SMOKY BACON IS THE PERFECT ADDITION TO THESE MELT-IN-THE-MOUTH SUGAR-TOPPED POTATOES.
THEY TASTE GREAT AS A CHANGE FROM ROAST POTATOES, WITH ROAST DUCK OR CHICKEN.

SERVES FOUR TO SIX

INGREDIENTS

   butter, for greasing
   900g/2lb sweet potatoes
   115g/4oz/½ cup soft light
     brown sugar
   30ml/2 tbsp lemon juice
   45ml/3 tbsp butter
   4 rashers (strips) smoked lean bacon,
     cut into matchsticks
   salt and ground black pepper
   1 flat leaf parsley sprig, to garnish

1 Preheat the oven to 190°C/375°F/ Gas 5 and lightly butter a shallow ovenproof dish. Cut each unpeeled sweet potato crosswise into three and cook in boiling water, covered, for about 25 minutes until just tender.

2 Drain and leave to cool. When cool enough to handle, peel and slice thickly. Arrange in a single layer, overlapping the slices, in the prepared dish.

5 The potatoes are ready once they are tender; test them with a knife to make sure. Remove from the oven once they are cooked.

6 Preheat the grill (broiler) to a high heat. Sprinkle the potatoes with parsley. Place the pan under the grill for 2–3 minutes until the potatoes are browned and the bacon is crispy. Serve hot.

3 Sprinkle over the sugar and lemon juice and dot with butter.

4 Top with the bacon and season well. Bake uncovered for 35–40 minutes, basting once or twice.

BAKED SWEET POTATO SALAD

THIS SALAD HAS A TRULY TROPICAL TASTE AND IS IDEAL SERVED WITH ASIAN OR CARIBBEAN DISHES.

SERVES FOUR TO SIX

INGREDIENTS
  1kg/2¼lb sweet potatoes
For the dressing
  45ml/3 tbsp chopped fresh coriander
    (cilantro)
  juice of 1 lime
  150ml/¼ pint/⅔ cup natural (plain)
    yogurt
For the salad
  1 red (bell) pepper, seeded and
    finely diced
  3 celery sticks, finely diced
  ¼ red skinned onion, finely chopped
  1 red chilli, finely chopped
  salt and ground black pepper
  coriander (cilantro) leaves, to garnish

1 Preheat the oven to 200ºC/400ºF/Gas 6. Wash and pierce the potatoes all over and bake in the oven for 40 minutes or until tender.

2 Meanwhile, mix the dressing ingredients together in a bowl and season to taste. Chill while you prepare the remaining ingredients.

3 In a large bowl mix the red pepper, celery, onion and chilli together.

4 Remove the potatoes from the oven and when cool enough to handle, peel them. Cut the potatoes into cubes and add them to the bowl. Drizzle the dressing over and toss carefully. Season again to taste and serve, garnished with fresh coriander.

ORANGE CANDIED SWEET POTATOES

ESPECIALLY POPULAR IN SOUTHERN US, NO THANKSGIVING TABLE IS COMPLETE UNLESS SWEET POTATOES ARE ON THE MENU. SERVE WITH EXTRA ORANGE SEGMENTS TO MAKE IT REALLY SPECIAL.

SERVES EIGHT

INGREDIENTS
 900g/2lb sweet potatoes
 250ml/8fl oz/1 cup orange juice
 50ml/2fl oz/¼ cup maple syrup
 5ml/1 tsp freshly grated ginger
 7.5ml/1½ tsp ground cinnamon
 6.5ml/1¼ tsp ground cardamom
 7.5ml/1½ tsp salt
 ground black pepper
 ground cinnamon, to garnish
 orange segments, to serve

1 Preheat the oven to 180°C/350°F/ Gas 4. Peel and dice the potatoes and then boil in water for 5 minutes.

2 Meanwhile, stir the remaining ingredients together. Spread out on to a non-stick shallow baking tin (pan).

3 Drain the potatoes and sprinkle them over the tin. Cook for 1 hour, stirring the potatoes every 15 minutes until they are tender and well coated. Serve as an accompaniment to a main dish, with extra orange segments and ground cinnamon to taste.

SPICED SWEET POTATO TURNOVERS

THE SUBTLE SWEETNESS OF THESE WONDERFUL PINK "POTATOES" MAKES A GREAT TURNOVER FILLING WHEN FLAVOURED WITH A SELECTION OF LIGHT SPICES.

SERVES FOUR

INGREDIENTS
For the filling
   1 sweet potato, about 225g/8oz
   30ml/2 tbsp vegetable oil
   2 shallots, finely chopped
   10ml/2 tsp coriander seeds, crushed
   5ml/1 tsp ground cumin
   5ml/1 tsp curry powder
   115g/4oz/1 cup frozen peas, thawed
   15ml/1 tbsp chopped fresh mint
   salt and ground black pepper
   mint sprigs, to garnish
For the pastry
   15ml/1 tbsp olive oil
   1 small egg
   150ml/¼ pint/⅔ cup natural (plain)
     yogurt
   115g/4oz/8 tbsp butter, melted
   275g/10oz/2½ cups plain (all-
     purpose) flour
   1.5ml/¼ tsp bicarbonate of soda
     (baking soda)
   10ml/2 tsp paprika
   5ml/1 tsp salt
   beaten egg, to glaze

1 Cook the sweet potato in boiling salted water for 15–20 minutes, until tender. Drain well and cool. When cool peel the potato and cut into 1cm/½in cubes.

2 Heat the oil in a frying pan, add the shallots and cook until softened. Add the sweet potato and fry until it browns at the edges. Add the spices and fry, stirring, for a few seconds. Remove the pan from the heat and add the peas, mint and seasoning to taste.

3 Preheat the oven to 200°C/400°F/ Gas 6. Grease a baking sheet. To make the pastry, whisk together the oil and egg, stir in the yogurt, then add the melted butter. Sift the flour, bicarbonate of soda, paprika and salt into a bowl, then stir into the yogurt mixture to form a soft dough. Turn out the dough, and knead gently. Roll it out, then stamp it out into rounds.

4 Spoon about 10ml/2 tsp of the filling on to one side of each round, then fold over and seal the edges.

5 Re-roll the trimmings and stamp out more rounds until the filling is used up.

6 Arrange the turnovers on the prepared baking sheet and brush the tops with beaten egg. Bake in the oven for about 20 minutes until crisp and golden brown. Serve hot, garnished with mint sprigs.

SWEET POTATO, PUMPKIN AND PRAWN CAKES

THIS UNUSUAL ASIAN COMBINATION MAKES A DELICIOUS DISH WHICH NEEDS ONLY A FISH SAUCE OR SOY SAUCE TO DIP INTO. SERVE WITH NOODLES OR FRIED RICE FOR A LIGHT MEAL.

SERVES FOUR

INGREDIENTS

200g/7oz/1⅓ cups strong white
  bread flour
2.5ml/½ tsp salt
2.5ml/½ tsp dried yeast
175ml/6fl oz/¾ cup warm water
1 egg, beaten
200g/7oz prawn (shrimp) tails, peeled
225g/8oz pumpkin, peeled, seeded
  and grated
150g/5oz sweet potato, grated
2 spring onions (scallions), chopped
50g/2oz water chestnuts, chopped
2.5ml/½ tsp chilli sauce
1 garlic clove, crushed
juice of ½ lime
vegetable oil, for deep-frying
lime wedges, to serve

1 Sift together the flour and salt into a large bowl and make a well in the centre. In a separate container dissolve the yeast in the water until creamy then pour into the centre of the flour and salt mixture. Pour in the egg and set aside for a few minutes until bubbles appear. Mix to form a smooth batter.

2 Place the prawns in a pan with just enough water to cover. Bring to the boil then reduce the heat and simmer for about 10 minutes. Drain, rinse in cold water and drain again well. Roughly chop then place in a bowl along with the pumpkin and sweet potato.

3 Add the spring onions, water chestnuts, chilli sauce, garlic and lime juice and mix well. Fold into the batter mixture carefully until evenly mixed.

4 Heat a 1cm/½in layer of oil in a large frying pan until really hot. Spoon in the batter in heaps, leaving space between each one, and fry until golden on both sides. Drain on kitchen paper and serve with the lime wedges.

SWEET POTATO FISH ROLLS

THE SWEETNESS OF THE POTATOES IS OFFSET PERFECTLY BY THE TARTNESS OF THE LEMON BUTTER SAUCE SERVED OVER THE FISH ROLLS.

SERVES FOUR

INGREDIENTS
   2 large sweet potatoes
   450g/1lb cod fillet
   300ml/½ pint/1¼ cups milk
   300ml/½ pint/1¼ cups water
   30ml/2 tbsp chopped parsley
   rind and juice of 1 lemon
   2 eggs, beaten
For the coating
   175g/6oz/3 cups fresh white
      breadcrumbs
   5ml/1 tsp Thai 7-spice seasoning
   vegetable oil, for frying
For the sauce
   50g/2oz/4 tbsp butter
   150ml/¼ pint/⅔ cup single (light)
      cream
   15ml/1 tbsp chopped fresh dill

1 Scrub the sweet potatoes and cook them in their skins in plenty of lightly salted boiling water for 45 minutes or until very tender. Drain and cool.

2 When the potatoes are cool, peel the skins and mash the flesh.

3 Place the cod fillet in a large frying pan and pour over the milk and water. Cover and poach for 10 minutes or until the fish starts to flake.

4 Drain and discard the milk, and then remove the skin and the bones from the fish.

5 Flake the fish into the potatoes in a large bowl, stir in the parsley, the rind and juice of ½ of the lemon and 1 egg. Chill for 30 minutes.

COOK'S TIP
Make sure the mixture is chilled thoroughly before you begin shaping and cooking. This helps to hold the ingredients together.

6 Divide and shape the mixture into 8 oval sausages. Dip each in egg. Mix the breadcrumbs with the seasoning. Roll the dipped fish rolls in the breadcrumbs.

7 Heat the oil and shallow fry in batches for about 7 minutes, carefully rolling the rolls to brown evenly. Remove from the pan and drain on kitchen paper. Keep hot.

8 To make the sauce, melt the butter in a small pan and add the remaining lemon juice and rind and allow the mixture to sizzle for a few seconds.

9 Remove from the heat and add the cream and dill. Whisk well to prevent the sauce from curdling and serve with the fish rolls.

SWEET POTATO BREAD WITH CINNAMON AND WALNUTS

A WONDERFUL BRUNCH DISH, AND COMPLETELY DELICIOUS SERVED WITH CRISPY BACON.

3 Drain the potato and cool in cold water, then peel the skin. Mash the potato with a fork and mix into the dry ingredients with the nuts.

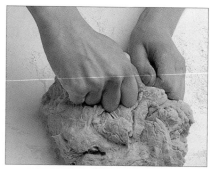

4 Make a well in the centre and pour in the milk. Bring the mixture together with a round-bladed knife, place on to a floured surface and knead for 5 minutes.

5 Return the dough to a bowl and cover with a damp cloth. Leave to rise for 1 hour or until doubled in size. Turn the dough out and knock back (punch down) to remove any air bubbles. Knead again for a few minutes. If the dough feels sticky add more flour to the mixture. Shape into a ball and place the bread in an oiled and base-lined 900g/2lb loaf tin (pan). Cover with a damp cloth and leave to rise in a warm place for 1 hour or until doubled in size.

6 Preheat the oven to 200°C/400°F/ Gas 6. Bake on the middle shelf of the oven for 25 minutes. Turn out and tap the base; if it sounds hollow the bread is cooked. Cool on a wire rack.

MAKES A 900G/2LB LOAF

INGREDIENTS
  1 medium sweet potato
  5ml/1 tsp ground cinnamon
  450g/1lb/4 cups strong white bread
    flour
  5ml/1 tsp easy-blend (rapid-rise) dried
    yeast
  50g/2oz/½ cup walnut pieces
  300ml/½ pint/1¼ cups warmed milk
  salt and ground black pepper

COOK'S TIP
For an extra-crispy loaf, after the bread is cooked, remove from the tin and return to the oven upside down on the oven rack. Cook for a further 5 minutes.

1 Boil the whole potato in its skin for 45 minutes or until tender.

2 Meanwhile, sift the cinnamon and flour together into a large bowl. Stir in the dried yeast.

SWEET POTATO AND HONEY BREAD ROLLS

A SWEET ROLL THAT TASTES AS DELICIOUS SERVED WITH CONSERVES AS WITH A SAVOURY SOUP.

MAKES TWELVE

INGREDIENTS

1 large sweet potato
225g/8oz/2 cups strong white bread
   flour
5ml/1 tsp easy-blend (rapid-rise)
   dried yeast
a pinch of ground nutmeg
a pinch of cumin seeds
5ml/1 tsp clear honey
200ml/7fl oz/scant 1 cup warm milk
oil, for greasing

1 Cook the potato in plenty of boiling water for 45 minutes or until very tender. Preheat the oven to 220°C/425°F/Gas 7.

2 Meanwhile, sift the flour into a large bowl and add the yeast, ground nutmeg and cumin seeds. Give the ingredients a good stir.

3 Mix the honey and milk together. Drain the potato and peel the skin. Mash the potato flesh and add to the flour mixture with the liquid.

4 Bring the mixture together and knead for 5 minutes on a floured surface. Place the dough in a bowl and cover with a damp cloth. Leave to rise for 30 minutes.

5 Turn the dough out and knock back (punch down) to remove any air bubbles. Divide the dough into 12 pieces and shape each one into a round.

6 Place the rolls on a greased baking sheet. Cover with a damp cloth and leave to rise in a warm place for 30 minutes or until doubled in size.

7 Bake for 10 minutes. Remove from the oven and drizzle with more honey and cumin seeds before serving.

COOK'S TIP
This dough is quite sticky, so use plenty of flour on the surface when you are kneading and rolling it.

SWEET POTATO MUFFINS WITH RAISINS

MUFFINS HAVE BEEN A PART OF THE AMERICAN BREAKFAST FOR MANY YEARS. THIS VARIETY MIXES THE GREAT COLOUR AND FLAVOUR OF SWEET POTATOES WITH THE MORE USUAL INGREDIENTS.

MAKES TWELVE

INGREDIENTS
    1 large sweet potato
    350g/12oz/3 cups plain
      (all-purpose) flour
    15ml/1 tbsp baking powder
    1 egg, beaten
    225g/8oz/1 cup butter,
      melted
    250ml/8fl oz/1 cup milk
    50g/2oz/scant ½ cup raisins
    50g/2oz/¼ cup caster
      (superfine) sugar
    salt
    icing (confectioners') sugar,
      for dusting

1 Cook the sweet potato in plenty of boiling water for 45 minutes or until very tender. Drain the potato and when cool enough to handle peel off the skin. Place in a large bowl and mash well.

2 Meanwhile, preheat the oven to 220°C/425°F/Gas 7. Sift the flour and baking powder over the potatoes with a pinch of salt and beat in the egg.

3 Stir the butter and milk together and pour into the bowl. Add the raisins and sugar and mix the ingredients until everything has just come together.

4 Spoon the mixture into muffin cases set in a muffin tin.

5 Bake for 25 minutes until golden. Dust with icing sugar and serve warm.

SWEET POTATO SCONES

THESE ARE SCONES WITH A DIFFERENCE. A SWEET POTATO GIVES THEM A PALE ORANGE COLOUR AND THEY ARE MELTINGLY SOFT IN THE CENTRE, JUST WAITING FOR A KNOB OF BUTTER.

2 In a separate bowl, mix the mashed sweet potatoes with the milk and melted butter or margarine. Beat well to blend.

3 Add the flour to the sweet potato mixture and stir to make a dough. Turn out on to a lightly floured surface and knead until soft and pliable.

MAKES ABOUT TWENTY-FOUR

INGREDIENTS
  butter, for greasing
  150g/5oz/1¼ cups plain
    (all-purpose) flour
  20ml/4 tsp baking powder
  5ml/1 tsp salt
  15g/½oz/1 tbsp soft light
    brown sugar
  150g/5oz mashed sweet potatoes
  150ml/¼ pint/⅔ cup milk
  50g/2oz/4 tbsp butter or
    margarine, melted

1 Preheat the oven to 230°C/450°F/ Gas 8. Grease a baking sheet. Sift together the flour, baking powder and salt into a bowl. Mix in the sugar.

4 Roll or pat out the dough to a 1cm/½in thickness. Cut into rounds using a 4cm/1½in cutter.

5 Arrange the rounds on the baking sheet. Bake for about 15 minutes until risen and lightly golden. Serve warm.

INDEX